"Religions do not have a
sionate or inclusive peopl
founders. We often empha
that actually change our l
cellent and much needed book, *Cultivating Compassion in an Interfaith World* will help bridge this gap."
    —**Fr. Richard Rohr, O.F.M.,** Center for Action and Contemplation, author of *The Naked Now* and *Everything Belongs*

"The major premise of this book is simple: Compassion is essential for both personal and our collective well-being and happiness. Using meditation as the particular instrument of personal transformation, Hliboki integrates the wisdom of Eastern and Western religious traditions as she guides us through a process for deepening our capacity for compassion. In doing so she draws attention to the essential ingredients for a transformation of consciousness—finding our center; addressing our illusions; realizing our inter-connectedness with all being; and experiencing the divine essence that flows through our relationships with self, others and nature. This contemplative consciousness is the life force of a compassion that has the power to transform the human condition. Realizing it answers any question or doubt about our true purpose in life."
    —**Robert G. Toth,** Past Executive Director, Merton Institute for Contemplative Living

---

"This is a beautiful, simple and open-hearted guide to contemplative practice. It contains much practical wisdom and will provide real support and encouragement to those seeking to live with greater compassion."
    —**Douglas E. Christie, Ph.D.,** Loyola Marymount University, author of *The Word in the Desert* and *The Blue Sapphire of the Mind*

"A wonderful comparison of the shared roots across religious traditions that lifts out the centrality of compassion. In concrete and inviting ways, *Cultivating Compassion in an Interfaith World* illustrates respect for each tradition while engaging the reader with creative suggestions to develop the practice of compassion within and across our traditions—a brilliant contribution to all of us concerned with finding ways to deepen our wells of kindness and build bridges across our many divides."

—**John Paul Lederach, Ph.D.,** Professor of International Peacebuilding, Kroc Institute, University of Notre Dame, author of *The Moral Imagination: The Art and Soul of Building Peace*

—————

"At a time when kindness may be interpreted as weakness, and when concern for others is often limited to messages in cyberspace, *Cultivating Compassion in an Interfaith World* demonstrates the beauty and peace that comes with an attitude of true compassion. Drawing from Islamic, Christian and Buddhist scriptures, it is a helpful resource for people of faith who wish to infuse their lives with the light of compassion."

—**Tayyibah Taylor,** Publisher & Editor-in-Chief, *Azizah Magazine*

—————

"Hliboki writes with palpable respect for three of the major faith traditions, identifying common ground but cherishing their distinctiveness. Pastors, retreat leaders or spiritual mentors who value the diversity of religious experience ought to be able to utilize her book as a guide and resource with minimal adaptation for varying circumstances or audiences. Hliboki looks both East and West, and in her book the twain meet."

—**Alexander Patico,** North American Secretary, Orthodox Peace Fellowship

"*Cultivating Compassion in an Interfaith World* is a wonderful sharing of experiences and meditations to lead one to the Beloved. I recommend it highly."

—**Aziza Scott,** head of the Esoteric School, Sufi Order International

———

"Scholars and teachers of the spiritual practice traditions of the world's great religions suggest that at the core of each of these streams of wisdom lies compassion—empathic feeling combined with appropriate, restorative action that brings life to individuals, communities, and the world. Julie Hliboki takes this assertion from the theoretical to the practical. She doesn't simply say we must be compassionate. Rather, she shows us how to cultivate compassion within ourselves for the benefit of all life. In this much-needed approach, Hliboki affirms the unique expressions of compassion found in three separate religious traditions, while helping us see and embrace their common center."

—**Andrew Dreitcer, M.Div., Ph.D.,** Executive Co-Director of the Center for Engaged Compassion, Claremont School of Theology, Claremont Lincoln University

———

"*Cultivating Compassion in an Interfaith World* captures the essence of compassion from different spiritual traditions showing us how common love is amongst all peoples. In spite of this, many people find it hard to practice compassion in their daily lives to others and to themselves. Hliboki's book presents practical contemplative spiritual exercises that can be easily taught to clinicians and others needing to integrate compassion into our own lives and helping them recognize the sacred in all we do. I strongly recommend this book to anyone searching for the sacred within and especially to those in the healing professions."

—**Christina M. Puchalski, MD,** Director, George Washington Institute for Spirituality and Health

"This book should grace the reading table of the spiritual seeker. In it the author moves us from a dual existence of 'right' 'wrong' 'up' 'down' to an interfaith world of promise and kindness. Hliboki teaches the way of compassion while educating us in the faith traditions. By offering practical steps for the journey, she makes our trek possible."

—**Frances Henry,** author of *Vaccines for Violence*

"Like a prism of light, *Cultivating Compassion in an Interfaith World* refracts the pure light of the Beloved into a gorgeous spectrum of possibilities. These serve as portals to remind us of the inexplicable immediacy of Divine Presence. The genius of this book is not only its vision but also how it calls the reader to take up spiritual practices that open the mind and heart to the radiant light of compassion. Be forewarned—these practices not only console but also call us to stretch beyond our comfort zones, to become larger than ourselves so that we might become who we truly are."

—**Rev. Robert V. Thompson,** author of *A Voluptuous God: A Christian Heretic Speaks*

"Hliboki has been blessed with a very precious spirituality, and she is, once again, moved to share it with us in a work that enriches the heart, mind, and soul. It is our prayer that God continues to bless her, and that she continues to publish these blessings."

—**Imam Plemon T. El-Amin,** Chair, Interfaith Community Initiatives

Also by the Author

The Breath of God:
Thirty-Three Invitations to Embody Holy Wisdom

Cultivating Compassion in an Interfaith World

99 Meditations to Embrace the Beloved

Julie Hliboki

Transilient Publishing

ISBN # 978-0-9832602-1-9

Library of Congress Control Number: 2012950571

Cover: "Mercy" by Julie Hliboki

For Carolyn,

a bodhisattva like no other

and

To all of you

who desire to embrace the Beloved

in yourself, in others, and

in all sentient beings.

May this book be a guide for you as you

cultivate compassion and become the invitation

that our complex, interfaith world so needs.

With deep gratitude, thank you.

Contents

Acknowledgments

My walk with the Beloved is a moment-to-moment journey. These moments string together, like pearls on a necklace, creating for me a reality that is filled with wonder, intimacy, and gratitude. My deepest connections, in both light and shadow, reveal the Divine gifts in myself, in others, and in all that exists. It is difficult, therefore, to identify and thank all those who have influenced my life and, as a result, this book. Friends, teachers, and guides—you know who you are and I am profoundly grateful for your presence.

Specifically, I wish to thank several people who contributed their talents to creating this book. Regina Kay provided thoughtful, skilled editing and insights as I attempted to express myself clearly. Karin Kinsey designed the beautiful cover and page layout. Countless others—including my dear friends Anita, Charlotte, and Matt—reviewed the work and offered words of encouragement to help move the project along.

Finally, I wish to thank my beloved, David, who embodies compassion. He is the love of my life, and our sacred journey together provides me continuous delight and joy.

Introduction

The Light of the Beloved

This book is an invitation to deepen into relationship with the Beloved through cultivating compassion. For me, the Beloved is personal, inter-personal, and trans-personal; that is, the Divine appears in many forms. I find the Beloved in myself, in others, and in all that exists. This innate connection to our Divine essence (Sufi), Christ-light (Christian), and Buddha-nature (Buddhist) lives in all and radiates from the core of every being. Cultivating compassion through contemplative practice connects us to our center, which in turn enables us to recognize and to connect to the essence of others.

Sufis speak about the Beloved as the Sun, the center of everything, burning brightly and feeding all life. The Ninety-Nine Names of God, or the attributes of the Beloved within the Qur'an, are the rays of light emanating from the sun. As these rays of light touch the stars, the earth, human beings, and other life forms, all are infused with light and the aspects of God. The entire world, and all its parts, become signs of the existence of the Beloved. We are engaged with this light-filled actuality every day. Simply to live, therefore, is to sense the Beloved's presence in everything and everyone.

Sufis also have a lovely way of describing how the Beloved resides within us. Within each of us is a lamp containing a brightly burning light, the illumination of the Beloved. Throughout the trials of childhood, we have learned fear and built defenses. This causes our lamps to become covered with dust or soot. Contemplative practice is a way of polishing our lamp. Meditating is like pulling out a dust rag and removing the layers of grime that cover our lamp. As we continue to polish our lamp a little each day, we reveal our light to others and ourselves.

The Verse of Light says:

> *Allah is the light of the heavens and the earth. His light is as a niche in the wall in which there is a lamp, the lamp is in a glass, and the glass is as it were a brightly shining star, lit from a blessed olive-tree, neither eastern nor western, the oil whereof appears to give light though fire touch it not. Light upon light! Allah guides to His light whom He pleases, and Allah sets forth parables for men, and Allah is Cognizant of all things.*
>
> —Qur'an, 24:35

Jesus says:

> *You are the light of the world. A city set on a hill cannot be hid. Nor do men light a lamp and put it under a bushel, but on a stand, and it gives light to all in the house. Let your light so shine before men, that they may see your good works and give glory to your Father who is in heaven.* —Matthew 5:14-16

Buddha says:

> *Just as treasures are uncovered from the earth, so virtue appears from good deeds, and wisdom appears from a pure and peaceful mind. To walk safely through the maze of human life, one needs the light of wisdom and the guidance of virtue.*

Sometimes our soul can be thought of as a mirror, which through suffering becomes covered with dust. We need to remove this layer of dust so that our soul can reflect the light of the Beloved's gifts. Comprehending the nature of suffering can help us recognize how our dust collects. Cultivating compassion will improve our luminosity.

A Primer on the Nature of Suffering

Our suffering often stems from wanting our lives to be different from what they are. We either hope that our situation will change or fear that it might never change. Rather than first accepting our circumstances as they exist, and then responding accordingly, hope and fear cloud our ability to see reality. We live in a state of uneasiness. Our response to life becomes defensive and controlling or helpless and withdrawing.

Another way we perpetuate our suffering is fear of loss. To counter this fear, we may attach ourselves to the intangible, such as our identity, beliefs, and attitudes. Or we may over-identify with the tangible, including our partner, job, or finances. Often people construe that these longed-for experiences or things are so important that we cannot survive without them.

Life is really a continuous flow of impermanence. In this ever-changing sea, our desire for predictability and permanence leaves us grasping for emotional life vests and locking onto whatever we believe will keep us safe. Unfortunately, often the very thing we are holding onto is unhealthy for us. We remain in harmful relationships, meaningless jobs, and engage in endless avoidance behavior just to evade change. The concept of impermanence—that every moment will be different from the next—is so frightening to us that we continue to agonize unnecessarily and cause distress to others. These behaviors undermine our natural tendency toward happiness.

The Role of Compassion

Etymologically, the word "compassion" is derived from two Latin words: *com,* which means "with" and *pati,* which means "suffer." Literally "compassion" means "to suffer with." Compassionate people make a commitment to free themselves and others from suffering and its causes in order to experience true happiness. Compassionate traits include love, affection, kindness, gentleness, generosity of spirit, and warm-heartedness. Practiced regularly, these traits move one out of the cycle of hope and fear, those emotions that perpetuate our distress. Exercising these traits can allow us to develop the very compassion that one is expressing.

Compassionate acts are also contagious and cause a wonderful ripple effect that extends far beyond the original act. If, for example, when I am driving, I allow a car to pull out in front of me, that driver may be impacted such that he enters his place of employment with a compassionate attitude toward a frustrating co-worker. I also feel better, and my sense of patience and compassion will likely influence me for the rest of the day.

Everyone has an inborn desire to overcome pain and be happy. When we cultivate compassion, we transform suffering into happiness. We experience deep connection and intimacy with the true nature of life. We feel better about ourselves, others, and the world.

Part One
Cultivating Compassion

While compassion plays an important role in all religions, this book focuses on the three faith traditions that I am most familiar with—Sufism, Christianity, and Buddhism. In this section, I speak to what Islamic, Christian, and Buddhist teachings say about compassion. I also share personal experiences that have resulted from my commitment to Sufi, Christian, and Buddhist contemplative practices.

Compassion within Islam

"Compassion" is the most frequently occurring word within the Qur'an, the holy book of Islam. Mercy, along with love, is the essence of Islam as expressed throughout the Qur'an. Ar-Rahman, the Most Compassionate, is the first among the Ninety-Nine Names of God, the characteristics of God within the Qur'an. The quality of compassion, as Ar-Rahman, opens each chapter: *b-ismi-llahi r-rahmani r-rahimi*. This invocation, "In the name of Allah, the Compassionate, the Merciful," begins the prayerful journey of reading and reciting Allah's message as conveyed through the Prophet Muhammad.

The Qur'an states more than three dozen times that there is only one God, "no God but He," and that God is compassionate.

And your God is one God! There is no god but He; He is the Compassionate, the Merciful.

—Qur'an, 2.163

Muslims are encouraged to call upon the compassionate God, to receive God's grace and mercy, to offer this love and empathy to those who are close to us, and to show patience and kindheartedness to others.

Call upon Allah or call upon the Compassionate God; whichever you call upon, He has the best names; and do not utter your prayer with a very raised voice nor be silent with regard to it, and seek a way between these.

—Qur'an, 17.110

And were it not for Allah's grace on you and His mercy, and that Allah is Compassionate, Merciful.

—Qur'an, 24.20

And one of His signs is that He created mates for you from yourselves that you may find rest in them, and He put between you love and compassion; most surely there are signs in this for a people who reflect.

—Qur'an, 30.21

Then he is of those who believe and charge one another to show patience, and charge one another to show compassion. —Qur'an, 90.17

The Compassionate God is the only source that creates order, provides the life force behind all that is, and sustains us in our daily life.

Who created the seven heavens one above another; you see no incongruity in the creation of the Compassionate God; then look again, can you see any disorder?

—Qur'an, 67.3

Have they not seen the birds above them expanding (their wings) and contracting (them)? What is it that holds them aloft save the Compassionate God? Surely He sees everything. Or who is it that will be a host for you to assist you besides the Compassionate God? The unbelievers are only in deception. —Qur'an, 67.19-20

Say: He is the Compassionate God, we believe in Him and on Him do we rely, so you shall come to know who it is that is in clear error. —Qur'an, 67.29

We also learn in the Qur'an that those who follow God's lead and live a compassionate life are known by their humbleness and are able to offer peace to others.

And the servants of the Compassionate God are they who walk on the earth in humbleness, and when the ignorant address them, they say: Peace. —Qur'an, 25.63

The Prophet of Islam embodied compassion. His life is filled with empathetic acts toward fellow human beings irrespective of their religions or stations in life. The following two well-known stories illustrate this:

Once a woman was brought to the Prophet accused of being a sinner and in need of punishment.

The Prophet, rather than asking her to expound on her sins, asked what acts of compassion she had done for others. She said, "I cannot recall any act of good towards any other human being." The Prophet again asked her whether she had helped any living being? The woman thought for a while and then said, "Once a dog was thirsty. He was near a water pit but unable to reach the water with his tongue. I took pity on the dog, took off my sock, fetched water from the pit, and gave it to the dog." The Prophet said, "Go! Allah will forgive all of your sins for this one act of mercy."

A woman used to throw garbage on the Prophet whenever he passed by her. One day, when no garbage was thrown, he inquired about the woman and was told she was ill. He went to her house to ask about her health, and when finding her sick, prayed for her recovery. Overwhelmed with this gesture of mercy by the Prophet, she converted to Islam.

Compassion is highly necessary for sustenance of life on this earth. The Qur'an levies a tithe on Muslims called *zakat,* which must be spent on disadvantaged sectors of society. The Prophet is reported to have said that it is more meritorious to feed a hungry widow than to pray an entire night.

Cultivating Compassion Through Sufism— Mandalas of Peace

My work with the Ninety-Nine Names Peace Project is one example of how Sufism has provided me a pathway to cultivate compassion. The project arose initially as a contemplative practice—painting each of the Ninety-Nine Names of God as *mandalas*. The Sanskrit word for circle, a *mandala* represents wholeness, and may be viewed as a model for the organizational structure of life itself—a cosmic diagram that reminds us of our relation to the infinite, the world that extends both beyond and within our body and mind.

The entire process began one afternoon while I was attending a silent Sufi retreat. I was walking a labyrinth on a sunny day and toning one of the Ninety-Nine Names of God—*Nur* or light—and a beautiful spherical image appeared. The energetic properties of this vision differed from my usual *mandala* experience. There was a deeper quality, so I stopped walking to sit with the sensations I was feeling in my body. When I closed my eyes, I saw an exhibit of peace-themed art.

The exhibit was in a foreign country, and patrons came from various religions with a common interest in sharing peace-centered communities. Its purpose was to build bridges of compassion, and to reduce suffering as only embracing the other makes possible. Throngs of individuals milled about sharing their appreciation of art and initiating conversations about peace. They were drawn by the artwork but remained for the conversations. I heard God's voice utter that I was to create and exhibit the Ninety-Nine Names of God.

That evening I approached the Sufi retreat leader who also directs the Esoteric School of the Sufi Order International. I spoke with her about the vision, explaining that I felt inadequate to undertake such a project since I knew so little about Sufism, Muslim traditions, and the Ninety-Nine Names. She invited me to pray with her. On concluding our prayer, she provided encouragement and permission to work with the Ninety-Nine Names. Later that night I spoke with the Beloved about my reluctance to take on the project and I rejected the calling. I felt something shut down in my body. For the next four years the call persisted, though I continued to reject it.

In 2008, a colleague told me, "A call from God persists." I realized that the one constant force in my life through the past eight years had been the Ninety-Nine Names project. I was perplexed. Could it be that the Beloved was still inviting me to realize my vision? Is that what God wanted for my life? The project still seemed too complex. Perhaps, in my desire to be led into God's desire for me, I was ready to trust the call. Questions flooded my mind.

Through prayer, discernment, and the encouragement of loved ones, I have since waded deeply into this process. This is my co-creative dance with the Divine. My willingness to be led through discerning God's will provides me with a sense of excitement, peace, and inspiration. I am grateful that I feel the Holy Spirit resonate in my body, that God speaks to me through visions, and that I have been granted a calling that combines contemplation, art, and peace.

Each of us hears the Beloved in our own way, and accesses compassion and wisdom through our own path. When I open to a name, a visual image of the name in the style of a *mandala* begins to appear. By creating an internal environment of openness, expansiveness, and receptivity in my body, I hold the space for the vision to fully materialize. The revelation of the *mandala* may take shape in seconds or gradually over a longer period. While the vision is developing, a physical vibration activates at the base of my skull and courses down my arms to my fingertips. It is energizing like an electrical current, yet is soft, gentle, and full, like water flowing gently in a stream. Centering myself in prayer, this current spills out of my hands onto the paper and I begin sketching the *mandala*.

I work with water-soluble pastels, pencils, and crayons arranged in tins and grouped by color. Often before I apply paint to a portion of a *mandala,* a color will either emanate from the paper or will appear brighter in the tins than the other colors, calling to me. Sometimes a color will visually vibrate in a tin. Other times I will hear an internal voice suggesting a color for a particular area. With a paintbrush I lift the pigment from the pastel, pencil, or crayon. I find this a delicate, meditative application that encourages patience, care, and listening at each step of the painting practice.

In painting the Ninety-Nine Names of God, I have a deep sense of awe and reverence for both the process of painting and for each created image. I pray that in sharing this process and journey, I will honor, express, and impart the love and beauty of the Beloved.

My book, *The Breath of God: Thirty-Three Invitations to Embody Holy Wisdom,* contains thirty-three of these *mandalas,* along with poetry, insights from the Abrahamic faiths, questions for reflection, and an invitation into a contemplative artistic practice for each quality featured in the book. The project has grown to include works from artists and poets besides me.

Compassion within Christianity

Within Christianity, many teachings speak of the importance of compassion. The Old and New Testaments contain seventy-five references to compassion and two hundred and thirty-six references to mercy (Revised Standard Version). In the Tanach, the Hebrew Scriptures, God reveals a compassionate nature and bestows this compassion widely:

> *And if he cries to me, I will hear, for I am compassionate.* —Exodus 22:27

> *The Lord is good to all, and his compassion is over all that he has made.* —Psalm 145:9

> *The compassion of man is for his neighbor, but the compassion of the Lord is for all living beings.*
> —Sirach 18:13

> *Yet thou hast dealt with us, O Lord our God, in all thy kindness and in all thy great compassion.*
> —Baruch 2:27

The importance of compassionate acts is recognized by fellow human beings, too, and often accompanied with gratitude and blessing:

> *And Saul said, "May you be blessed by the Lord; for you have had compassion on me."* —1 Samuel 23:21

The common Orthodox Trisagion prayer speaks of God as "everywhere present and filling all things."

> *O Heavenly King, Comforter, Spirit of Truth, Who are everywhere present and filling all things, Treasury of blessings and Giver of life: Come and dwell in*

us, and cleanse us of all impurity, and save our souls, O Good One.

In the New Testament, God is spoken of as the "Father of mercies" and the "God of all comfort." God bestows his compassion on those who are suffering and provides comfort. Those who witness his example are familiar with suffering and understand the importance of offering empathy and comfort to others.

Blessed be the God and Abba of our Lord Jesus Christ, the parent of mercies and God of all comfort, who consoles us in all our affliction, so that we may be able to reassure those who are in any affliction, with the consolation with which we ourselves are comforted by God. For as we share abundantly in Christ's sufferings, so through Christ we share abundantly in solace too. If we are afflicted, it is for your relief and salvation; and if we are comforted, it is for your ease, which you experience when you patiently endure the same sufferings that we suffer. Our hope for you is unshaken; for we know that as you share in our sufferings, you will also share in our comfort.

—2 Corinthians 1:3–7 (modified RSV)

Jesus embodies for Christians the very essence of mercy. The Gospels are filled with his compassionate acts, teachings, and parables.

As he went ashore he saw a great throng, and he had compassion on them, because they were like sheep without a shepherd; and he began to teach them many things.

—Mark 6:34

Jesus Feeds the Crowds

> *Then Jesus called his disciples to him and said, "I have compassion on the crowd, because they have been with me now three days, and have nothing to eat; and I am unwilling to send them away hungry, lest they faint on the way." And the disciples said to him, "Where are we to get bread enough in the desert to feed so great a crowd?" And Jesus said to them, "How many loaves have you?" They said, "Seven, and a few small fish." And commanding the crowd to sit down on the ground, he took the seven loaves and the fish, and having given thanks he broke them and gave them to the disciples, and the disciples gave them to the crowds. And they all ate and were satisfied; and they took up seven baskets full of the broken pieces left over. Those who ate were four thousand men, besides women and children.* —Matthew 15:32–38*

Jesus Raises the Dead

> *As he drew near to the gate of the city, behold, a man who had died was being carried out, the only son of his mother, and she was a widow; and a large crowd from the city was with her. And when the Lord saw her, he had compassion on her and said to her, "Do not weep." And he came and touched the bier, and the bearers stood still. And he said, "Young man, I say to you, arise." And the dead man sat up, and began to speak. And he gave him to his mother.* —Luke 7:12–15*

Jesus assures his listeners in the Sermon on the Mount that, "Blessed are the merciful, for they shall obtain mercy."

Seeing the crowds, he went up on the mountain, and when he sat down his disciples came to him. And he opened his mouth and taught them, saying:

"Blessed are the poor in spirit, for theirs is the kingdom of heaven.

"Blessed are those who mourn, for they shall be comforted.

"Blessed are the meek, for they shall inherit the earth.

"Blessed are those who hunger and thirst for righteousness, for they shall be satisfied.

"Blessed are the merciful, for they shall obtain mercy.

"Blessed are the pure in heart, for they shall see God.

"Blessed are the peacemakers, for they shall be called sons of God.

"Blessed are those who are persecuted for righteousness' sake, for theirs is the kingdom of heaven.

—Matthew 5:1–10

Jesus offers several parables to his followers, challenging them to forsake their own desires and to act compassionately towards others, particularly those in need or distress. In the Parable of the Prodigal Son, Jesus teaches that the compassionate, forgiving father welcomes his wayward son home with unconditional love. Likewise, God as the merciful and forgiving parent, embraces and loves us when we err.

And he said, "There was a man who had two sons; and the younger of them said to his father, 'Father, give me the share of property that falls to me.' And he divided his living between them. Not many days later, the younger son gathered all he had and took his journey into a far country, and there he squandered his property in loose living. And when he had spent everything, a great famine arose in that country, and he began to be in want. So he went and joined himself to one of the citizens of that country, who sent him into his fields to feed swine. And he would gladly have fed on the pods that the swine ate; and no one gave him anything. But when he came to himself he said, 'How many of my father's hired servants have bread enough and to spare, but I perish here with hunger! I will arise and go to my father, and I will say to him, "Father, I have sinned against heaven and before you; I am no longer worthy to be called your son; treat me as one of your hired servants."'

And he arose and came to his father. But while he was yet at a distance, his father saw him and had compassion, and ran and embraced him and kissed him. And the son said to him, 'Father, I have sinned against heaven and before you; I am no longer worthy to be called your son.' But the father said to his servants, 'Bring quickly the best robe, and put it on him; and put a ring on his hand, and shoes on his feet; and bring the fatted calf and kill it, and let us eat and make merry; for this my son was dead, and is alive again; he was lost, and is found.' And they began to make merry. —Luke 15:11–24

In the Parable of the Good Samaritan, Jesus holds up to his followers the ideal of compassionate conduct.

But he, desiring to justify himself, said to Jesus, "And who is my neighbor?" Jesus replied, "A man was going down from Jerusalem to Jericho, and he fell among robbers, who stripped him and beat him, and departed, leaving him half dead. Now by chance a priest was going down that road; and when he saw him he passed by on the other side. So likewise a Levite, when he came to the place and saw him, passed by on the other side. But a Samaritan, as he journeyed, came to where he was; and when he saw him, he had compassion, and went to him and bound up his wounds, pouring on oil and wine; then he set him on his own beast and brought him to an inn, and took care of him. And the next day he took out two denarii and gave them to the innkeeper, saying, 'Take care of him; and whatever more you spend, I will repay you when I come back.' Which of these three, do you think, proved neighbor to the man who fell among the robbers?" He said, "The one who showed mercy on him." And Jesus said to him, "Go and do likewise." —Luke 10:29–37

True Christian compassion, say the Gospels, should extend to all, even to the extent of loving one's enemies.

But love your enemies, and do good, and lend, expecting nothing in return; and your reward will be great, and you will be sons of the Most High; for he is kind to the ungrateful and the selfish. —Luke 6:35

Cultivating Compassion Through Christianity— Healing Light

Between my deep contemplative practice and my openness to the transforming Christ-light, I have had more than a dozen profound experiences with Jesus that focus on cultivating compassion. The following is one recent encounter that speaks to the essence of Jesus as a source of compassion and the resurrection as an end to suffering.

I am on the fourth day of a silent retreat. After a series of practices that include purification breathing, attunement to light, and sacred chants, the instructions read: "What Being arrives for you? What gift is the Being offering you? Breathe the gift into your heart then give it out to the world."

The Being that comes to me is Jesus. He opens his right hand, extended toward me, palm up. In his hand is a ball of radiating light. The light doesn't leave his hand, but reaches me nonetheless, penetrates my heart and then fills the rest of my body. I soak it in and then beam it back to the world, intending it to reach every receptive nook and cranny.

I am a beacon of light; such is my purpose. I am a light for the Beloved that burns away the darkness and moves toward awareness, awakening, and unity. The light, this Christ-light, comes from God, enters me, and radiates out from me. I need do nothing but be receptive and open to it, allowing it to pour into me, through me, connecting all to oneness in light. I need not extend any effort sending it anywhere. The light will find the receptive openings on its own, the nooks and crannies that have cracked open to let it in, all the broken places, all the fractured crevasses, all the expanded hearts. It is not my job to find where the light goes, merely to participate in the process of its moving.

This is grace, the ever-pervading light that shines regardless of whether we acknowledge it, take it in, learn from it, heal with it, and awaken to it. The light is also within us, within our lamps, our lamps waiting to be polished so that we can shine even more brightly. Immanent and transcendent, within and without, both supporting each other, seeking each other in connection and communion.

The light is the stuff of love sitting in the former wound of Jesus' hand. Or, is love made manifest through light? The sustenance of love radiates into all things through light. Without this light/love, all would cease to exist. It is our nourishment, our pathway, and our key to awakening.

Am I willing to let this light, this love, burn away anything that is in its way, anything that interferes with its shining more brightly, moving more freely, or exchanging with the Beloved more seamlessly? This light, which is my soul, is so much bigger than my body. It is ever pervading, it connects beyond the physical into the realm of oneness. All I need is to be open and receptive and willing to respond in the exchange.

How does this beam of love want to manifest itself in the world through me? How can I best be a beacon and share the exchange? What is the path of least resistance? To what compassionate action is it calling me? I believe it is in aligning myself with those offerings that allow more light to enter me—relationships, professions, creativity, attitude, practices—those things that make my heart sing with joy. I need to stay in tune with the light/love, and my unique light by polishing my lamp, so that I can see where it is leading me.

The light is not sitting on the top of Jesus' palm, but is emanating out of the wound created in his hand, the hole left from the crucifixion. The light/love that fills his body pours out through the opening left from the wound, from his profound suffering. Do our wounds create such openings? Do my wounds, those that feel as though they will never heal, serve such a purpose? Do they provide an avenue for light and love to pour through to others, an opening or crack that allows me to shine, to give, all that more brightly?

It doesn't matter to Jesus whether the wound is still physically painful. Its purpose has shifted into an extraordinarily powerful one—that of God's mark, not God's wound or as though God wounded (since the wounds were caused by the ignorance of human beings, the stuff of shadow not fully integrated or brought into the light for examination). The wound, which IS, no longer takes in darkness but instead manifests light. It has been transformed through the resurrection, healed into a portal that is receptive to connection, to unity, to healing on all levels, in all manners, with all sentient beings. It becomes the embodiment of compassion, a pathway to heal all suffering.

My wounds, some of which I believed will never heal or close, can remain open without continuing to cause me pain. They are transformed into a new kind of intelligence, fresh receptors that allow me to respond with more wisdom, compassion, and truth to what is. I do not need to reopen them to hear their message of past lessons. I need not cling in fear to these old patterns for protection from future hurt. I do not need to feel the pain to remind myself that this was not good for me. Rather, the wounds have healed open, not for the purpose of being able to look into them, but to let love and light through them, to be a source of compassion and healing for others as well as me. I want to carry these wounds differently, not as crucifixion but as resurrection.

When I imagine my body in this condition it looks like Swiss cheese with holes everywhere. These are wounds ubiquitous, emanating light/love. Will I lose too much light and love through so many openings? Is that possible? Are the holes also a place for light and love to enter? It doesn't feel as though I will lose more than I gain. I need not worry that I will be depleted.

I believe the light is generated within my heart and infused through my *chakras*. All of the pores in my body are receptive to absorbing the light/love from the Beloved. The wounds are one place it comes out, but not the only place.

I ebb and flow back and forth between a crucified and resurrected order. How am I feeding these states? I want my wounds to shift into a resurrected condition, out of their painful crucified form, so that they are portals for love, for healing the world, for beaming the Christ-light energy. This will take practice, a shift in consciousness, the polishing of my internal lamp, openness and receptivity to God's leading, continual awakening, and shifting from fear to faith. It will take remembrance of the Beloved's compassion.

Compassion within Buddhism

My understanding of compassion as a response to the nature of suffering began about twenty years ago with Buddhism, specifically with Pema Chodron's teaching of the *tonglen* meditation. The *tonglen* practice is a method for connecting with suffering—both within others and ourselves—and awakening the compassion that is inherent in all of us. At the core of the practice, one breathes in the pain or suffering of another so that they can be well. Then one breathes out relaxation and happiness to that person in order to send him or her relief and joy. I began practicing this meditation of receiving suffering and sending happiness before I knew much else about Buddhism, and found the practice to be deeply transformative. *Tonglen* also helped me understand the concept of dependent co-arising—that what arises in the complexity of life is dependent on multiple causes and conditions.

About ten years ago, I added the *Metta,* or Loving-kindness, meditation to my practice. *Metta* begins with cultivating loving-kindness for oneself, then loving-kindness toward loved ones, friends, community, strangers, enemies, and, finally, all sentient beings. Many Buddhists and non–Buddhists alike find the Loving-kindness practice to be profoundly moving as a method for cultivating compassion. The contemplative compassion practices within this book are based on the *Metta* meditation format.

More recently, I have begun the practice of *zazen* (literally meaning "seated practice") and the study of core Buddhist teachings. Within the Zen tradition, the aim of *zazen* is to allow thoughts, words, images, and ideas to arise and fall away without the practitioner becoming attached to them. By focusing on the breath, noticing how it arises and falls away without effort, one can, likewise, eventually learn to let distractions pass by without effort. With practice comes a greater ability to concentrate, to remain present in the moment, and to embrace reality.

Learning to be present, and to respond to life's unfolding in each moment, has helped me understand the core principles of Buddhism including the nature of suffering, impermanence, and dependent co-arising. The teachings of the Four Noble Truths, the Eightfold Path, and the Sixteen Precepts (Zen Peacemaker Order) provide a wonderful groundwork from which to cultivate compassion.

The Four Noble Truths

The teachings on the Four Noble Truths explain the nature of suffering, its causes, and how it can be overcome. In summary, the Four Noble Truths are:

- Suffering exists.
- The origin of this suffering is our delusion or ignorance.
- The cessation of suffering is possible.
- Following the Eightfold Path will end suffering.

Dukkha is the Buddhist term commonly translated as "suffering." It can also mean stress, anxiety, dissatisfaction, or out of balance. The emphasis on suffering is not intended to be pessimistic, but rather to identify the nature of suffering, and a means to overcome it.

Our distress often stems from the fact that everything that exists is temporary. We prefer to live with the illusory mindset that things are permanent, controllable, and predictable rather than accepting their true nature of impermanence. We want to believe that if we hold on tightly enough to things—both tangible (people, possessions, jobs) and intangible (identities, beliefs, ideas)—we can keep ourselves from experiencing loss. This craving for and clinging to eternalness is the root cause of our suffering. Everything will come to pass. Until we can accept this, we will continue to suffer.

The cessation of suffering is cultivated by learning how to intersect with life in a different way, one that is free from craving and clinging. Meditation practices help with this process, and the Eightfold Path is a guideline to end the path of suffering. This path of self-improvement gradually reduces our cravings, ignorance, and delusions, and allows us to live with greater awareness, peace, and joy.

The Eightfold Path

The Eightfold Path is organized into three divisions: wisdom, ethical conduct, and concentration. Wisdom includes right view and right intention; ethical conduct includes right speech, right action, and right livelihood; and concentration includes right effort, right mindfulness, and right concentration. The eight "right" items of the path are not to be understood as stages, in which each stage is completed before moving on to the next. Rather, they are to be understood as eight significant dimensions of one's behavior that are interdependent. Taken together, they define a complete path, or way of living.

Right view means seeing things as they really are, acknowledging the Four Noble Truths, and understanding the impermanent nature of objects and ideas. Since our view of the world forms our thoughts and actions, right view leads to ethical conduct.

Right intention means committing to renunciation of attachment, freedom from ill will, and doing no harm. More specifically, right intention calls for relinquishing craving, feelings of anger and aversion, and thinking or acting aggressively. Rather, right intention encourages the development of a compassionate attitude.

Right speech refers to abstaining from lying, from divisive language, from abusive discourse, and from idle chatter. Phrased positively, this means to tell the truth, to speak warmly and in a friendly manner, and to talk only when necessary.

Right action involves bodily actions and refers to refraining from unwholesome deeds. This aspect asks that we abstain from doing harm, taking life, stealing, and illicit sex or sexual misconduct. We are to act compassionately, nurture life, live honestly, respect the belongings of others, and to ensure sexual relationships are non-exploitative.

Right livelihood means that one should earn one's living in an honorable way and that wealth should be gained legally and peacefully.

Right effort abandons all of our wrong and harmful thoughts, words, and deeds. It encourages us to prevent the arising of unwholesome states, to abandon these circumstances, to arouse healthy forms that have not yet taken place, and to manifest, maintain, and perfect nourishing conditions.

Right mindfulness asks us to be conscious, reflective, and deliberate, making sure we do not act or speak due to inattention or forgetfulness.

Right concentration cultivates wholesome thoughts and actions through the practice of meditation. This concentration enables us to remain present to what is arising in the present moment.

The Three Refuges of a Zen Peacemaker

Inviting all of creation into the *mandala* of my practice and vowing to serve them, I take refuge in the:

- Buddha, the awakened nature of all beings;
- Dharma, the ocean of wisdom and compassion;
- Sangha, the community of those living in harmony with all Buddhas and Dharmas.

The Three Tenets of a Zen Peacemaker

Taking refuge and entering the stream of engaged spirituality, I vow to live a life of:

- Not-knowing, thereby giving up fixed ideas about myself and the universe;
- Bearing witness to the joy and suffering of the world;
- Loving action, healing myself and others.

The Ten Practices of a Zen Peacemaker

Being mindful of the interdependence of Oneness and Diversity, and wishing to actualize my vows, I engage in the spiritual practices of:

- Recognizing that I am not separate from all that is. This is the precept of Non-Killing.
- Being satisfied with what I have. This is the precept of Non-Stealing.
- Encountering all creations with respect and dignity. This is the precept of Chaste (or pure) Conduct.

- Listening and speaking from the heart. This is the precept of Non-Lying.

- Cultivating a mind that sees clearly. This is the precept of Not Being Deluded.

- Unconditionally accepting what each moment has to offer. This is the precept of Not Talking About the Errors and Faults of Others.

- Speaking what I perceive to be the truth without guilt or blame. This is the precept of Not Elevating Oneself and Not Blaming Others.

- Using all of the ingredients of my life. This is the precept of Not Being Stingy.

- Transforming suffering into wisdom. This is the precept of Not Being Angry.

- Honoring my life as an instrument of peacemaking. This is the precept of Not Thinking Ill of the Three Refuges.

Cultivating Compassion Through Buddhism—Holding My Seat

I first heard the phrase "holding your seat" from Roshi Fleet Maul, a priest within the Zen Peacemaker Order and Shambala Buddhist traditions. I was attending one of his retreats at Upaya Zen Center on the topic of "Radical Responsibility." In addition to the imagery of staying seated on my cushion—a known place that allows me to explore the unknown of groundlessness—the phrase speaks to resourcing oneself and developing resiliency. Resourcing is the process of turning to the Beloved, the Source, for whatever resource one needs in order to respond skillfully to the present moment. The contemplative practice of sitting *zazen* has helped me learn how to "hold my seat."

There are many ways that we become unseated, meaning that we feel triggers, might become reactive, and may well withdraw. One way we unseat ourselves centers on the issue of judgment, shame, and blame. When we judge, shame, or blame another, we link our wellbeing or our self-worth to something or someone outside of ourselves. By such an attitude, we are essentially conveying the message, "You need to be different in order for me to be OK, so I am going to try to manipulate and control you either through force or withdrawal."

We may feel that we are powerful through the process of trying to control, but we are actually giving up our power and reinforcing for ourselves that we are powerless. We are acting as if we are helpless if the world does not conform to our judgments. We are telling ourselves that the resources we have to respond to any given situation are not enough, and we are, in turn, actually judging, shaming, and blaming ourselves.

Through this process, we undermine our own field of stability, our resource base, and our innate sensibility. We feel isolated, abandoned, without protection, and we look for someone to blame for our discomfort. This starts the whole darn cycle over again. Wow.

I have learned that I can hold my seat in difficult situations. When I allow the emotions to wash over me without getting stuck in them, I find that I can resist the trigger of going to judgment, shame, and blame, whether of myself or others. From this position, I am resourced and can respond authentically from a place of centeredness rather than fear. I find I can establish clearer boundaries without feeling isolated, experience compassion, care for others and me, and operate from a stable platform. I am better able to discern my options. I ask myself, "How will I choose to respond to this?"

My contemplative practice helps me enormously in "holding my seat," remaining grounded when I feel as though things are spinning out of control. Every day I practice sitting with what is and how I might respond from that position. This means allowing my thoughts, emotions, and distractions to wash over me and dissipate, arising and falling away, just like the breath. Resourcing me in this way reinforces compassion for others and myself.

Another area that unseats us is our perception of what provides security and what creates insecurity. Over the past few months, I have been exploring in depth the Bhagavad Gita. I am deeply moved by its message, which is to follow your authentic, true calling no matter what and let go of the fruits of however this calling manifests itself in the world. In other words, be your true, divine self in all that you do and let go of the outcome.

And how does one discern an authentic true calling and step into the divine self? According to the Gita and most works of wisdom, it is through contemplative practice that one becomes aware of one's deeper, truer and, even, divine self. By listening to our still small voice in meditation, we learn to differentiate the self-protective and security-seeking demands of the ego from one's true self. It is by such practice that we begin to make changes in the way we interact with others and even alter our relationships with ourselves. Some changes are drastic and some are subtle. What they have in common is that they are leading us toward truth, creating a real sense of security inside us that we can return to again and again. With practice, we learn to live in truth, by doing our best and letting go of trying to control the outcome.

Yes, we get startled and become afraid, and yes, we have our reaction. How long we stay in that reaction is up to us. Contemplative practice helps us more quickly to come back to our center, to our seat, to our true place of security. Rather than merely having reactions, we come to have responses. We experience something, discern our response, and move forward in peace, stability, and safety. We also learn to let go of all those unhealthy attitudes, relationships, and situations that we have been holding on to. We realize that—rather than providing us security—they are actually draining our life energy.

Another way we can hold our seat is through compassion, especially self-compassion. For example, I have become aware at a deeper level about my desire to heal several unhealthy, long-term thought patterns. Specifically, I have been examining my fear of experiencing eventual loss of those I love and hold most dearly. I dread what I fear would be resulting unbearable pain. Of course I *know* that we will all die, me included, so in a very real sense I *will* lose everyone. How I face and deal with this fact, however, makes all the difference in my ability to handle the eventual loss.

My fear (and old pattern of thinking) is that loss is a form of punishment, that unbearable pain is deserved, and that when I am hurting I will be utterly abandoned to suffer on my own. Although I have come a long way in healing and changing this perspective, I have had some new insights while sitting *zazen*. I have realized that in my most seemingly unbearably painful moments, in my darkest times, I have broken open into a cavernous experience of Love. In my fractured state, I have found a deeper, more profound light than I had known existed. In this light, I have felt held and supported by the Beloved, a benevolent power so strong that I knew nothing could break this connection. Even if I turned away in shame or pain or anguish, I would still be sustained by Love.

Yet in moments of fear, I still doubt, I still feel that disconnection and abandonment is possible. This is where compassion comes in. I am compassionate with myself for the doubt, for the vigilance that still creeps in, for the moments when fear takes over. I am recognizing that I am still in the healing process. Perhaps it will take my lifetime. That is OK. I am grateful for my courage to face the fears, my desire to transform my perspective, and for my contemplative practice that sustains me each day. As much as I would like to be rid of all of the past gunk, these memories are in my cells. Healing takes time. Gentleness is required.

Contemplative practices such as *zazen,* teach us to hold our seats while in the midst of triggers, fear, pain, and doubt. They are a doorway into love, joy, equanimity, and compassion for others and the self. I invite you to learn to hold your seat as you walk your path and awaken into being.

Part Two
Embracing the Beloved

Each meditation in this book is an invitation to embrace the Beloved—in you, in others, and in the world—through intentionally cultivating compassion. They draw upon the compassionate, mystical heart of my three faith traditions—Sufism, Christianity, and Buddhism. The meditations are inspired by and organized around the theme of the Ninety-Nine Names of God, those characteristics by which Muslims regard Allah. The names come from the Qur'an, the Islamic holy book. Some of the same qualities of the Beloved are also found within the Bible and other sacred texts.

Compassion is the first of the Ninety-Nine Names of God. In my experience, it is the doorway that opens and enables me to embody the other ninety-eight attributes. As I cultivate compassion for others and me, I develop a greater sense of becoming more human. I am better able to see the characteristics of the Beloved within those I encounter and to honor our commonalities and differences within relationships. This portal opens a pathway to wisdom, mercy, truth, justice, and the rest of the attributes, all necessary ingredients for meaningful engagement with life. Cultivating compassion connects me with my own sacredness and, from this starting point, propels me to do what I can to make a difference in the world.

Each of the ninety-nine meditations presented in this volume focuses on a particular attribute of the Beloved. Each is comprised of verses from the book of Psalms, a prayer for support, a compassion meditation, and a question for reflection. For me, the Psalms are a call to and a response from a compassionate God. The Psalm verses flow back and forth between the longing for the relief of suffering and the experience of that relief from the Beloved. In this prayerful engagement, we are able to deepen into our understanding of what it means to be human. An intimacy emerges with the Beloved, a further discovery of that divine essence which connects us to ourselves, to each other, and to all.

The compassion meditations follow the format of the Buddhist *Metta* Loving-kindness practice. I have found this ritual to align my heart, mind, and soul into a unified, beneficent force. I am able to cultivate the resources required to energetically hold others and me in a state of wellbeing. This leads me to an actively engaged connection with the Beloved in all. It encourages a dynamic commitment to the world.

I invite you to work with these contemplative practices to cultivate compassion for yourself and others.

Working with the Contemplative Practices

The contemplative practices within this book offer a variety of ways to deepen into self-awareness. This will also foster compassion, gratitude, and interconnectedness. The following are a few examples of how you may wish to engage these practices.

Choosing a Quality of the Beloved to Guide You

There are several options for how to choose which quality will guide you on any given day. The initial option is to select the first of the ninety-nine qualities of the Beloved, Compassion (Ar-Rahman). Then each day advance in order on to the next attribute. Following this pattern, on day two work with the next aspect, which is Mercy (Ar-Rahim). On the third day, work with Universal Rule (Al-Malik), on the fourth day, Holy (Al-Quddus), and continue on in this fashion.

An alternative choice is to allow the Beloved, through that still small voice inside you, to guide your selection. To follow this path, first sit for a few minutes in silence with your eyes closed breathing slowly and focusing your attention on your breath. Allow your mind and body to relax, and when you are ready, ask the question, "Which quality will I benefit most from today?" With eyes closed, allow your hands to open the book to a page to see which characteristic is revealed.

A third possibility is to select a quality that attends to your particular need for that day. For example, if you are sensing a need for greater wisdom, turn to the page for Wisdom (Al-Hakim). If you are suffering and in need of comfort, you may wish to select the element of Healing (Ar-Rauf), or Falling (Al-Muntaqim), or another aspect of the Beloved that aids your understanding and movement towards wholeness.

Preparing for Contemplative Practice

Once you have selected a focus for today's contemplative practice, you are ready to begin your meditative journey with the Beloved.

Find a quiet, comfortable place to sit that will support you on your journey into silence. This may be in the corner of a bedroom or another nook in your home. If you do not already have a favorite meditation spot, you may wish to try various options to discover which one works best for you.

Sit on a chair, a cushion, the ground, or any other place that will allow you to be comfortable with your back straight for a period of twenty to thirty minutes.

Without leaning against a backing, position yourself with your spine erect. If you are seated in a chair, plant both feet flat on the floor. If you are seated cross-legged on a cushion, shift your weight around and make any slight adjustments in your posture in order to feel balanced and stable. In either position, rest your hands in your lap or on your knees.

Close your eyes and take several slow, deep breaths. Shift all of your focus to each inhale and exhale. Notice the rhythm of your body and the effortlessness of each breath rising and falling on its own. Allow your body and your mind to relax.

As streams of thought arise, allow them to move on without attaching to them or getting caught in a particular notion. To help with this process, one possibility is to imagine placing your distractions on leaves floating down a stream. Take each impression as it comes to you, and imagine yourself gently and lovingly placing it on a leaf to be carried away by the water. Another possibility is to image your thoughts as having wings. As each thought arises, picture it sprouting wings and taking flight.

The idea is to acknowledge your emerging preoccupations, just as you noticed your rising breath, and allow each idea to find its own ending, just as you noticed your falling breath. As your breath has its own rhythm, so do your thoughts. With time you will discover that as quickly as an impression arises it will fall away effortlessly so long as you do not attach yourself to it.

The same is true with our feelings. As you are sitting, emotions or emotional content may arise. Welcome and acknowledge them, and allow them to move on during your meditation time. Trust that anything important enough to demand your attention will present itself again to you after your meditation is complete. If a particularly strong emotion arises, you do not need to stop your contemplative practice to address it. Rather, invite the emotion into your meditation by asking yourself, "What is the Beloved trying to reveal to me?" Then notice what arises for you such as any insights or bodily sensations. If you desire, continue to follow those insights or sensations by asking again, "What is the Beloved presenting to me?" You may wish to have a journal nearby to document what you learned or experienced after your practice time.

Sit in silence for a few minutes longer engaged with the rising and falling of your breath.

Beginning the Contemplative Practice

Now that you have chosen a quality for your meditation, and have sat quietly for a few minutes, you are ready to begin the contemplative practice.

Reciting the Sacred Name

I recommend that you begin your contemplative practice by reciting the sacred name or quality of the Beloved you have chosen. When we pray a quality or name, Al-Hakim (Wisdom) for example, we use "Ya" (meaning O, as in to call someone) in front of the name rather than "Al," "Ar," "At," "An," or "As." So, Ya-Hakim (Wisdom), or Ya-Rahman (Compassion).

One option for reciting a sacred name is to say the word slowly aloud on each exhalation. Inhale deeply, and exhale Ya-Hakim. As you repeat this prayer, imagine silently inhaling the quality, in this case, that of Wisdom. As you breathe out, say the name aloud. Imagine offering the quality in prayer to all those who might benefit from receiving it. Inhale Wisdom, exhale Ya-Hakim to all. Continue in this fashion for a few minutes.

A second option for reciting a sacred name is to follow the Sufi tradition. In this ritual, when reciting a sacred name in prayer, we repeat the sacred name eleven, thirty-three, or one hundred and one times. If you have chosen the quality of Wisdom, for example, you would say Ya-Hakim either eleven, thirty-three, or one hundred and one times.

You may wish to create a string of beads for yourself to keep track of the number of times you say a name. I have a string of beads that holds ninety-nine beads divided into three segments, having thirty-three beads in each segment. The ninety-nine beads, plus the two divider beads, create one hundred and one beads. The first eleven beads of the first segment of thirty-three beads are different from the rest so that I can keep track of saying the name only eleven times if I wish.

A third option for reciting a sacred name is through toning. Toning refers to producing a sustained pitch with your voice, either by humming or by holding short vowel sounds. The tone may be so quiet as to be imperceptible to anyone other than you or it may be louder. Such a resonance creates a vibration that releases tension and encourages relaxation on the physiological level. It can draw your awareness deep within your body, providing an opportunity for sensing your essence, perceiving a spiritual oneness, and opening to healing.

As you intone the name of the Beloved, such as Al-Hakim (Wisdom), As-Salaam (Peace), or As-Sabur (Patience) for example, you may hum or sing a short vowel sound for that quality—pronounced AH (as in far), EH (as in end), EE (as in see), OH (as in own), or OU (as in you). For Al-Hakim, tone the "a" and "i" vowels—AH, EE. For As-Salaam, tone the "a" vowels—AH AH. For Ya-Sabur, tone the "a" and "u" vowels —AH OU. As you tone a name, note whether and where you feel a resonance in your body. Do your hands tingle? Does your chest or head vibrate?

You may also try toning the name itself. Or, you might select two names: one to tone as you inhale, the other to tone when you exhale. When toning the names, again use "Ya" in front of the name. One of my favorite pairs is Ya-Rahman (O Compassion) on the in-breath and Ya-Hakim (O Wisdom) on the out-breath. This meditative practice of compassion and wisdom coincides for me with the Zen notion of "soft front" and "strong back."

Reciting the Psalms and Prayer for Support

After reciting or toning the sacred name for several minutes, the next step is to engage the Psalm verse and prayer associated with the quality you have chosen. Read the Psalm verse slowly and mindfully and then allow for a moment of silence. Read through it a second time, then close your eyes and sit quietly for a few minutes with what you have read. Allow the words to penetrate your being and listen for any inner message. When you are ready, open your eyes and read through it a third time aloud followed by the prayer for support. Or, if you choose, you may read the verse and offer your own prayer. Again, close your eyes and sit in silence.

Reciting the Compassion Metta Prayers

Begin by making any slight adjustments to your posture so that you are comfortable. Using the compassion meditation for the quality you have chosen, start with the first line, which offers compassion to yourself. (If you find that it is too difficult to begin with yourself, start with the second line, which offers compassion to those you love.) After each offered prayer, have a moment of silence.

For example, continuing with the quality of Wisdom, recite the prayer:

May I embrace your divine wisdom.

Next, for those you love, recite the prayer:

May all those I love embrace your divine wisdom.

Next, for those in your community, recite the prayer:

May those in my community embrace your divine wisdom.

Next, for those whom you are struggling with or whom you fear, recite the prayer:

May those who I am struggling with or fear embrace your divine wisdom.

Next, for all sentient beings everywhere throughout the universe, recite the prayer:

May all beings embrace your divine wisdom.

As you recite the prayers, you may choose to recount each line once or eleven times. Or, you may choose to recite the prayer once, and then offer ten specific prayers for individuals. For example, using the Wisdom prayer for community, you might say:

May those in my community embrace your divine wisdom.

May the bus driver embrace your divine wisdom.

May Sarah's teacher embrace your divine wisdom.

May the bagger at the grocery store embrace your divine wisdom.

May my best friend's aunt embrace your divine wisdom.

…and so on.

Using the Wisdom prayer for all sentient beings, you might say:

May all beings embrace your divine wisdom.

May all wildlife embrace your divine wisdom.

May the flowers embrace your divine wisdom.

May the stars embrace your divine wisdom.

May the universe embrace your divine wisdom.

...and so on.

When you have finished reciting the compassion *Metta* prayers, continue to sit until your meditation feels complete. When you are done, open your eyes and slowly take in what you see in front of you while you are still sitting. Notice if any insights arise for you. You may wish to jot these down in your journal before standing up and attending to other activities for the day.

99 Meditations

Compassion
Ar-Rahman

Dearly Beloved, you are good to all, and your
compassion flows over and through all that you
have made. Everything that comes from you
embodies mercy and compassion.
Psalm 145:9–10

Help me to share mercy and compassion
freely with others.

———

O Beloved...
May I show compassion to me.
May I show compassion to all those I love.
May I show compassion to those in my community.
May I show compassion to those
I struggle with or fear.
May I show compassion to
all beings.

———

How might you offer compassion today to
someone in your life?

Mercy
Ar-Rahim

You, my Beloved, are gracious and
merciful, slow to anger and abounding
in unconditional love.
Psalm 145:8

Help me to recognize your absolute mercy,
and to offer this same mercy to others.

———

O Beloved…

May I bestow mercy upon me.
May I bestow mercy upon all those I love.
May I bestow mercy upon those
in my community.
May I bestow mercy upon those
I struggle with or fear.
May I bestow mercy upon all beings.

———

What does mercy feel like to you?

Universal Rule
Al-Malik

Let the heavens be glad, and let the earth rejoice; let the sea roar, and all that fills it; let the field exult, and everything in it! Then shall all the trees of the wood sing for joy before my Beloved, for you come to rule the earth with righteousness and truth.

Psalm 96:11–13

Help me to enter the universal interconnectedness of all and to celebrate nature's order.

———

O Beloved…
May I feel interconnected.
May all those I love feel interconnected.
May those in my community feel interconnected.
May those I struggle with or fear feel interconnected.
May all beings feel interconnected.

———

How do you recognize universal connection?

Holy

Al-Quddus

J know that you, my Beloved, are holy! You
made me, and J am yours; we are your
people, and the sheep of your pasture.

Psalm 100:3

Help the holy in me find and celebrate the
holy in another.

———

O Beloved...
May I see the holy in me.
May I see the holy in all those I love.
May I see the holy in my community.
May I see the holy in those I struggle with or fear.
May I see the holy in all beings.

———

How do you celebrate the holy?

Peace

As-Salaam

In peace I will both lie down and sleep;
for you alone, my Beloved, assure that all
is well and safe and good.

Psalm 4:8

Help me to relax and find peace within my
body, mind, and soul.

———

O Beloved...

May I sense internal peace.
May all those I love sense internal peace.
May those in my community sense internal peace.
May those I struggle with or fear sense
internal peace.
May all beings sense internal peace.

———

How does peace feel to you?

Security

Al-Mumin

J will sing of your unwavering love, my
Beloved, forever; with my mouth J will
proclaim your faithfulness to all
generations. For your unconditional love
was established ever more, your
faithfulness is secure as the heavens.

Psalm 89:1–2

Help me to find security in your love for me,
and to extend that faith and security
to all those J meet.

———

O Beloved…

May I be a rock of security for me.
May I be a rock of security for all those I love.
May I be a rock of security for my community.
May I be a rock of security for those I
struggle with or fear.
May I be a rock of security for all beings.

———

How do you experience security?

Guardian
Al-Muhaymin

Guard my life, my Beloved, for I am under
your care; I trust in you to help me. You are
my guardian; care for me as I cry out in need.
Gladden my soul, for to you do I offer
up all of my burdens.
Psalms 86:2–4

Help me to feel your presence guarding and
holding me particularly in times of distress.

———

O Beloved…
May I feel your guardian presence.
May all those I love feel your guardian presence.
May those in my community feel your guardian presence.
May those I struggle with or fear feel
your guardian presence.
May all beings feel your guardian presence.

———

How might you be a guardian for others
and yourself?

Self-Sufficiency
Al-Aziz

Dearly Beloved, you desire truth in my
inward being; therefore teach me wisdom in
my secret heart.
Psalm 51:6

Help me to find my way and discern my life
with your wisdom as my guide.

———

O Beloved...
May I develop wise self-sufficiency.
May all those I love develop wise self-sufficiency.
May those in my community develop wise self-sufficiency.
May those I struggle with or fear develop
wise self-sufficiency.
May all beings develop wise self-sufficiency.

———

How might you develop a greater sense of
self-sufficiency?

Compulsion
Al-Jabbar

In my angst, my heart became hot within me, the fire burned, and then I spoke: "Dearly Beloved, let me know how long I have to participate in this world."
Psalm 39:3–4

Help me to appreciate how fleeting my life is so that I may engage the present moment fully.

———

O Beloved…
May I fully appreciate the present moment.
May all those I love fully appreciate the present moment.
May those in my community fully appreciate
the present moment.
May those I struggle with or fear fully appreciate
the present moment.
May all beings fully appreciate the present moment.

———

What are you experiencing right now in this present moment?

Greatness

Al-Mutakabbir

J will call to mind your deeds, my Beloved;
yes, J will remember your wonders of all time.
J will meditate on all your gifts, and muse on
your mighty deeds. You are great
and your way is holy.
Psalm 77:11–13

Help me to reflect your greatness in
all that J do.

———

O Beloved…
May I celebrate the greatness in me.
May I celebrate the greatness in all those I love.
May I celebrate the greatness in my community.
May I celebrate the greatness in those
I struggle with or fear.
May I celebrate the greatness in all beings.

———

How do you embody greatness?

Perfect Order
Al-Khaliq

Your eyes beheld my unformed substance,
my Beloved; in your book of creation, each of
my days were formed for me in perfect order,
when as yet the days did not exist.
Psalm 139:16

Help me understand the dependent arising in
each moment and the contingency of my
being with all others.

———

O Beloved…

May I live into your perfect order.
May all those I love live into your perfect order.
May those in my community live into your perfect order.
May those I struggle with or fear live
into your perfect order.
May all beings live into your perfect order.

———

How do you recognize divine order?

Right-living
Al-Bari

In you, my Beloved, all is in order, all is
perfect, reviving my soul; your testimony is
sure, making me wise yet simple; your
precepts demonstrate right-living, rejoicing my
heart; your guidance is pure, enlightening
my eyes; my awareness of you is clean,
enduring forever; your order is true,
and good altogether.
Psalm 19:7–9

Help me to recognize and abide
by right-living.

———

O Beloved…
May I benefit from right-living.
May all those I love benefit from right-living.
May those in my community benefit from right-living.
May those I struggle with or fear benefit from right-living.
May all beings benefit from right-living.

———

How does it feel when you are participating
in right-living?

Beauty

Al-Musawwir

In your hand, my Beloved, are the depths
of the earth; the heights of the mountains are
also yours. The sea is yours, for you made it;
for your hands formed the dry land, you have
shaped the beauty of all.
Psalm 95:4–5

Help me to recognize my own beauty and to
perceive the beauty in others.

———

O Beloved...
May I recognize the beauty in me.
May I recognize the beauty in all those I love.
May I recognize the beauty in my community.
May I recognize the beauty in those I struggle with or fear.
May I recognize the beauty in all beings.

———

How do you recognize beauty within yourself
and others?

Forgiveness
Al-Ghaffar

Hear my cry, my Beloved, listen to my prayer;
from the end of the earth J call to you, when
my heart is faint. Lead me to the rock where
J will find forgiveness; for you are my refuge,
forgiving all, and strengthening me.
Psalm 61:1–3

Help me to forgive, be gentle, and offer
compassion to all including myself.

———

O Beloved…
May I forgive and offer compassion to me.
May I forgive and offer compassion to all those I love.
May I forgive and offer compassion to those
in my community.
May I forgive and offer compassion to those
I struggle with or fear.
May I forgive and offer compassion to all beings.

———

What is required for you to forgive yourself?

Force
Al-Qahhar

You are great, my Beloved, and abundant in
power, the ultimate force behind all life; your
understanding of my frailty is beyond measure.
Psalm 147:5

Help me to become aligned with your power
so that I may become a force for your love
in the world.

———

O Beloved...
May I become a force for your divine love.
May all those I love become a force for your divine love.
May those in my community become a force
for your divine love.
May those I struggle with or fear become
a force for your divine love.
May all beings become a force for your divine love.

———

How can you become a force for good?

Blessings
Al-Wahhab

Only for you, my Beloved, do I wait; for I
know it is you, the one who bestows all
blessings, who will answer and
provide what I need.
Psalm 38:15

Help me to receive your many gifts in the
blessings you present me in each moment.

———•———

O Beloved...
May I accept your blessings.
May all those I love accept your blessings.
May those in my community accept your blessings.
May those I struggle with or fear accept your blessings.
May all beings accept your blessings.

———•———

What are the blessings in your life?

Breath

Ar-Razzaq

You breathed your word, my Beloved, and the
heavens were made. All their host, everything
of this precious universe, are created and
sustained by your breath.
Psalm 33:6

Help me to feel your breath sustaining me.

———

O Beloved...
May I feel sustained by you.
May all those I love feel sustained by you.
May those in my community feel sustained by you.
May those I struggle with or fear feel sustained by you.
May all beings feel sustained by you.

———

What does sustaining breath feel like to you?

Opening
Al-Fattah

When you give to me, my Beloved, I gather
and absorb your blessings; when you open
your hand, I am opened, and filled with
your love and goodness.
Psalm 104:28

Help me to open to your light and love, and to
channel this into the world.

———

O Beloved...
May I open my light and love to me.
May I open my light and love to all those I love.
May I open my light and love to those in my community.
May I open my light and love to those
I struggle with or fear.
May I open my light and love to all beings.

———

How do you open to light?

Knowing

Al-Alim

When I am afraid, I put my trust in you, my
Beloved, trusting without fear. You know
everything, and in that understanding I find
strength to handle anything that
comes my way.
Psalm 56:3–4

Help me to lean on you when faced with a
difficult situation, and to know deep in my
bones that your love is ever present.

———

O Beloved…
May I be a knowing presence to me.
May I be a knowing presence to all those I love.
May I be a knowing presence to those in my community.
May I be a knowing presence to those
I struggle with or fear.
May I be a knowing presence to all beings.

———

What are a few things that you know
deeply in your bones?

Constriction
Al-Qabid

Dearly Beloved, I am feeling constricted, and
I do not wish to hide my challenges from you.
For when I confess that I am struggling,
I become open to your grace, and
this eases my constriction.
Psalm 32:5

Help me to become fully aware of when I am
contracting, and to release this tension
into your hands.

———

O Beloved...

May I be awakened through my experience of constriction.
May all those I love be awakened through their
experience of constriction.
May those in my community be awakened through their
experience of constriction.
May those I struggle with or fear be awakened through
their experience of constriction.
May all beings be awakened through
their experience of constriction.

———

What creates constriction for you?

Expansion
Al-Basit

You show me the path of life, my Beloved;
in your presence there is fullness of joy,
expansion of spirit, and relief of difficulties.
Your hands bestow blessings for evermore.
Psalm 16:11

Help me to comprehend the expansive
nature of all that I am.

———

O Beloved…
May I explore my expansiveness.
May all those I love explore their expansiveness.
May those in my community explore their expansiveness.
May those I struggle with or fear
explore their expansiveness.
May all beings explore their expansiveness.

———

What areas of your life are expanding?

Emptiness
Al-Khafid

Dearly Beloved, J remember what has gone before, and J meditate on all that you have done for me; J muse on what your hands have created, the entire universe. J am humbled. J stretch out my hands to you, and my soul desires you like a desert thirsts for rain.

Psalm 143:5–6

Help me to transform my perception of emptiness from one of loneliness to one of unlimited space and freedom.

———

O Beloved...

May I grow from my loneliness into freedom.
May all those I love grow from their
loneliness into freedom.
May those in my community grow from their
loneliness into freedom.
May those I struggle with or fear
grow from their loneliness into freedom.
May all beings grow from their
loneliness into freedom.

———

How does emptiness feel to you?

Exaltation
Ar-Rafi

Dearly Beloved, your faithfulness and your
unconditional love are with me always, and
these blessings exalt me.

Psalm 89:24

Help me to share my exaltation by elevating
all who J encounter.

———•———

O Beloved...
May my words elevate me.
May my words elevate all those I love.
May my words elevate those in my community.
May my words elevate those I struggle with or fear.
May my words elevate all beings.

———•———

How do you elevate others?

Honoring

Al-Muizz

Dearly Beloved, to honor my friends and
companions I will bestow the greetings,
"As-Salaam Alaikum, Peace be upon you,
and Shalom Aleichem!"
Psalm 122:8

Help me to impart honor and peace upon all
who I engage.

———

O Beloved...
May I impart honor and peace upon me.
May I impart honor and peace upon all those I love.
May I impart honor and peace upon
those in my community.
May I impart honor and peace upon those
I struggle with or fear.
May I impart honor and peace upon all beings.

———

Who in your life is in need
of honor and peace?

Humility
Al-Mudhill

When I look at your heavens, the work of
your fingers, the moon and the stars which you
have established, my Beloved, I am deeply
humbled. I am insignificant compared to this
vast universe, yet you are mindful of me and
care for me. You remind me of my
uniqueness and importance.
Psalm 8:3–4

Help me to understand at all times that
I am both a drop in the ocean and
the ocean itself.

O Beloved…
May I humble myself.
May I humble myself with all those I love.
May I humble myself with those in my community.
May I humble myself with those I struggle with or fear.
May I humble myself with all beings.

How do you show humility?

All Hearing

As-Sami

Give ear, my Beloved, to my prayer; hearken
to my cry of supplication. In the day of my
trouble I call on you, for you answer me.

Psalm 86:6–7

Help me to hear the cries of others and to
listen for your guidance in my response.

———

O Beloved...

May you hear my cries.
May you hear the cries of all those I love.
May you hear the cries of those in my community.
May you hear the cries of those I struggle with or fear.
May you hear the cries of all beings.

———

Who needs to be heard by you?

All Seeing
Al-Basir

Where could I go, my Beloved, where you
would not see me? Where could I flee and not
find your presence? If I ascend to heaven,
you are there. If I make my bed in the
shadows, you see me. If I took to the sky or
entered the depths of the ocean, you would
see me, your hand would lead me
and hold me.

Psalm 139:7–10

Help me to enter your light when I most want
to hide, to open to your love when I most want
to flee, and to see with the clarity
with which you see.

———

O Beloved...
May I see with clarity.
May all those I love see with clarity.
May those in my community see with clarity.
May those I struggle with or fear see with clarity.
May all beings see with clarity.

———

When do you see the most clearly?

Arbitration

Al-Hakam

For not from the east nor from the west and
not from the wilderness comes lifting up; but it
is you, my Beloved, who settles through
arbitration, putting down one and lifting up
another until both are in balance.
Psalm 75:6–7

Help me to recognize the authenticity of all
perspectives, as well as the incompleteness of
every position, especially my own.

———

O Beloved…
May I fully appreciate my perspectives.
May I fully appreciate the perspectives of all those I love.
May I fully appreciate the perspectives of those
in my community.
May I fully appreciate the perspectives of those
I struggle with or fear.
May I fully appreciate the perspectives of all beings.

———

What positions are you holding as complete?

Justice

Al-Adl

Dearly Beloved, you embody both unconditional
love and faithfulness, and divine
law and justice.
Psalm 89:14

Help me to always balance justice with love.

———

O Beloved…

May I balance justice with love for me.
May I balance justice with love for all those I love.
May I balance justice with love for those
in my community.
May I balance justice with love for those
I struggle with or fear.
May I balance justice with love for all beings.

———

What areas of your life require justice and
what areas love?

Gentleness

Al-Latif

Hear me, my Beloved, when I cry aloud and
be gracious to me and answer me with your
gentleness. You have said, "Seek my face."
My heart says to you, "Your face do I seek."
Psalm 27:7–8

Help me to be gentle as I seek your face
everywhere and to discover you in both the
subtle and the obvious.

———

O Beloved…
May I be gentle with me.
May I be gentle with those I love.
May I be gentle with those in my community.
May I be gentle with those I struggle with or fear.
May I be gentle with all beings.

———

Where do you need to be gentle with yourself?

Awareness
Al-Khabir

Search me, my Beloved, and know my heart.
Explore me and know my body, mind, and
soul. And see if there be any part of me that
remains unaware, and lead me to the full
consciousness of your love.
Psalm 139:23–24

Help me to embrace your love and to share it
unconditionally with all.

———

O Beloved…
May I feel the embrace of your divine love.
May those I love feel the embrace of your divine love.
May those in my community feel the embrace
of your divine love.
May those I struggle with or fear feel the embrace
of your divine love.
May all beings feel the embrace of your divine love.

———

What steps might you take today to increase
your awareness of divine love?

Reprieve

Al-Halim

My heart holds fast to your path, my Beloved,
my feet have returned me to you once again. I
call upon you when I need a respite, for you
answer me; incline your ear to me, hear my
words. Wondrously show your unconditional
love for me as I seek reprieve
from my struggles.

Psalm 17:5–7

Help me to provide a refuge to others through
unconditional love, acceptance,
and compassion.

———

O Beloved…
May I offer reprieve to me.
May I offer reprieve to those I love.
May I offer reprieve to those in my community.
May I offer reprieve to those I struggle with or fear.
May I offer reprieve to all beings.

———

What areas of your life need reprieve?

Magnificence
Al-Azim

I have felt your magnificence, my Beloved,
in nature. Awe during thunderstorms, when
clouds pour out water; the skies give forth
thunder; arrows flash on every side.
Reverence during your roar in the whirlwind;
lightening that lights up the world; when the
earth trembles and shakes.
Psalm 77:16–18

Help me to realize that the energy that flows
through nature also flows through me.

———

O Beloved...
May I embrace my magnificence.
May all those I love embrace their magnificence.
May those in my community embrace their magnificence.
May I those I struggle with or fear
embrace their magnificence.
May all beings embrace their magnificence.

———

How does the magnificence of nature
reveal itself to you?

Releasing Imperfections
Al-Ghafur

My steps are from you, my Beloved, and you
establish me in ways that delight you; though I
fall, you hide my faults, and release my
imperfections, so that I continue standing
with your steady support.

Psalm 37:23–24

Help me to be gentle with myself and others
when faults and imperfections
seem to dominate.

———

O Beloved…

May I release my perceived imperfections.
May all those I love release their perceived imperfections.
May those in my community release
their perceived imperfections.
May those I struggle with or fear release
their perceived imperfections.
May all beings release their perceived imperfections.

———

What imperfections in your life need releasing?

Gratitude
Ash-Shakur

I will give thanks to you, my Beloved, with my
whole heart; I will tell of all your wonderful
ways that touch me deeply each day. I will
be glad and exult in your love, and I will sing
praises that express my gratitude.
Psalm 9:1–2

Help me to remember how much joy I
receive from being grateful.

———

O Beloved…
May I be grateful for me.
May I be grateful for all those I love.
May I be grateful for those in my community.
May I be grateful for those I struggle with or fear.
May I be grateful for all beings.

———

In what ways do you express gratitude?

Highest Good
Al-Ali

J praise you, my Beloved, and everything that
you have made praises you, too. The sun and
moon praise you, and all of your shining stars.

Psalm 148:2–3

Help me to experience the heights of my love
and goodness, and to sing your
praises in gratitude.

————

O Beloved...

May I see the highest good in me.
May I see the highest good in all those I love.
May I see the highest good in my community.
May I see the highest good in those I struggle with or fear.
May I see the highest good in all beings.

————

How do you recognize the highest goodness
in yourself and others?

Grandeur

Al-Kabir

J and all the earth worship you, my Beloved;
J sing praises to you, sing praises to your
grandeur. J see your splendor: you are
the greatest of all.

Psalm 66:4–5

Help me to embrace all that unfolds in my life
as a gift from you, both the light and the
shadow, as they will illuminate my path.

———

O Beloved…
May I integrate my light and shadow.
May all those I love integrate their light and shadow.
May those in my community integrate
their light and shadow.
May those I struggle with or fear integrate
their light and shadow.
May all beings integrate their light and shadow.

———

What are your greatest gifts?

Preservation

Al-Hafiz

In your arms, my Beloved, I lie down and
sleep; I wake again, for you have sustained
me and preserved my life.

Psalm 3:5

Help me to preserve the lives of those beings
around me and to express gratitude upon
awakening each day.

———

O Beloved...

May I preserve my preciousness.
May all those I love preserve their preciousness.
May those in my community preserve their preciousness.
May those I struggle with or fear preserve
their preciousness.
May all beings preserve their preciousness.

———

What do you preserve?

Nourishment
Al-Muqit

Dearly Beloved, you uphold all who are
falling, and raise up all who are bowed down.
My eyes look to you, and you give me all the
nourishment I require in due season. Through
your open hand, you satisfy the desire
of every living thing.
Psalm 145:14–16

Help me to soak in and fully receive the
nourishment you provide in so many ways.

———

O Beloved...
May I receive your nourishment.
May all those I love receive your nourishment.
May those in my community receive your nourishment.
May those I struggle with or fear receive your nourishment.
May all beings receive your nourishment.

———

In what ways do you give and
receive nourishment?

Stewardship

Al-Hasib

One thing I ask of you, my Beloved, is that I
may dwell in your heart all the days of my life,
to behold the beauty of your stewardship, and
to seek your shelter. For you shield me during
my times of trouble; you account for me and
set me in a place of stability.

Psalm 27:4–5

Help me to recognize your presence
everywhere and to be a good steward of all
that is entrusted to me.

———

O Beloved…

May I embrace the practice of stewardship.
May all those I love embrace the practice of stewardship.
May those in my community embrace
the practice of stewardship.
May those I struggle with or fear embrace
the practice of stewardship.
May all beings embrace the practice of stewardship.

———

What is in need of your stewardship?

Majestic

Al-Jalil

Dearly Beloved, I will meditate upon the
glorious splendor of your majesty, and on your
wondrous works. I will declare your greatness
and share your abundant goodness, and sing
aloud of all that you bestow upon me.

Psalm 145:5–7

Help me to recognize the blessings of each
moment and to share all that I
have with others.

———

O Beloved…

May I recognize each majestic moment.
May all those I love recognize each majestic moment.
May those in my community recognize
each majestic moment.
May those I struggle with or fear recognize
each majestic moment.
May all beings recognize each majestic moment.

———

How do you celebrate majestic moments?

Generous

Al-Karim

May you, my Beloved, grant me my heart's
desire, and in your generosity,
fulfill all of my plans!
Psalm 20:4

Help me to be grateful for all that I receive
and to give generously to others of my time,
resources, and love.

———•———

O Beloved...
May I receive and give generously.
May all those I love receive and give generously.
May those in my community receive and give generously.
May those I struggle with or fear
receive and give generously.
May all beings receive and give generously.

———•———

Who is in need of your generosity?

Watchful

Ar-Raqib

Dearly Beloved, you look down from heaven,
and see everything; you are watchful over all
the inhabitants of the earth; you fashion my
heart, and observe my deeds.

Psalm 33:13–15

Help me to feel your presence watching over
me and all those who cross my path.

———

O Beloved...

May I sense your watchful presence.
May all those I love sense your watchful presence.
May those in my community sense your watchful presence.
May those I struggle with or fear
sense your watchful presence.
May all beings sense your watchful presence.

———

Who is in need of your watchfulness?

Listening
Al-Mujib

Let me hear, my Beloved, what you are
saying, for you are speaking peace to all who
turn their hearts toward you.

Psalm 85:8

Help me to listen for the response to my
heart-felt prayers.

———

O Beloved...

May I hear your response to my prayers.
May all those I love hear your response to their prayers.
May those in my community hear your
response to their prayers.
May those I struggle with or fear hear
your response to their prayers.
May all beings hear your response to their prayers.

———

How do you know your prayers
have been heard?

Vast

Al-Wasi

Whom have I in heaven but you, my Beloved,
you who comprehend all. There is nothing
upon earth that I desire besides you. My flesh
and my heart will fail one day, but you remain
now and forever as the strength of all that
is in this vast universe.

Psalm 73:25–26

Help me to call upon your vast and unending
love when I need strength and to share
this love freely.

———

O Beloved…

May I recognize your vast love.
May all those I love recognize your vast love.
May those in my community recognize your vast love.
May those I struggle with or fear recognize your vast love.
May all beings recognize your vast love.

———

How do you experience vastness?

Wisdom

Al-Hakim

Dearly Beloved, how manifold are your works!
In wisdom you have made them all; the
earth is full of your creatures.

Psalm 104:24

Help me to center my life with
your guiding wisdom.

———

O Beloved...

May I embrace your divine wisdom.
May all those I love embrace your divine wisdom.
May those in my community embrace your divine wisdom.
May those I struggle with or fear embrace
your divine wisdom.
May all beings embrace your divine wisdom.

———

What are the sources of wisdom for you?

Loving
Al-Wadud

Dearly Beloved, you love me so! You know when I sit down and when I rise up; you discern my thoughts from afar. You search out my path and where I sleep, and are acquainted with all my ways. Even before a word is on my tongue, you know it altogether. You surround me and lay your loving hands upon me. Knowledge of such a deep love is almost more than I can bear.

Psalm 139:1–6

Help me to open to the depths of your love and to share that love generously with others.

———

O Beloved…

May I offer encompassing love to me.
May I offer encompassing love to all those I love.
May I offer encompassing love to those in my community.
May I offer encompassing love to those
I struggle with or fear.
May I offer encompassing love to all beings.

———

Who in your life needs to be loved totally?

Glorious

Al-Majid

The heavens are telling the glory of you, my
Beloved; and the sky shows your handiwork.
The day pours forth your majesty and the
night declares its knowledge of you. Without
words, their voice goes out through all the
earth, and your glorious ways extend
to the end of the world.

Psalm 19:1–4

Help me to extol the glories of all who
I encounter.

———

O Beloved...

May I appreciate the glorious nature of me.
May I appreciate the glorious nature of those I love.
May I appreciate the glorious nature of
those in my community.
May I appreciate the glorious nature of those
I struggle with or fear.
May I appreciate the glorious nature of all beings.

———

How do you express glory?

Resurrection
Al-Baith

J have trusted in your unwavering love, my
Beloved, which has continuously renewed me;
my heart rejoices in your gifts. J will sing to
you, because you have resurrected
me time and again.
Psalm 13:5–6

Help me to know that there is a light at the
end of the tunnel and to feel your love
guiding the way.

———

O Beloved…

May I experience resurrection through your love.
May all those I love experience resurrection
through your love.
May those in my community experience resurrection
through your love.
May those I struggle with or fear experience resurrection
through your love.
May all beings experience resurrection through your love.

———

What does resurrection feel like
or mean to you?

Witness

Ash-Shahid

Open my lips, my Beloved, and my mouth
shall witness to you through praise.
Psalm 51:15

Help me to be a witness and ambassador for
compassion everywhere.

O Beloved…

May I be a witness to compassion for me.
May I be a witness to compassion for all those I love.
May I be a witness to compassion for
those in my community.
May I be a witness to compassion for
those I struggle with or fear.
May I be a witness to compassion for all beings.

How can you be a witness for others?

Truth

Al-Haqq

Make me to know your ways, my Beloved;
teach me your paths. Lead me in your truth,
and teach me, for you are the light of truth;
for your wisdom I wait all the day long.

Psalm 25:4–5

Help me to dedicate myself to the light of truth
and to walk your path with intention.

———

O Beloved…

May I discover and live your truth.
May all those I love discover and live your truth.
May those in my community discover and live your truth.
May those I struggle with or fear discover
and live your truth.
May all beings discover and live your truth.

———

What truths are you ignoring?

Dependable

Al-Wakil

But you, my Beloved, are a shield about me,
my trustee, and the one J can depend on. You
lift my head high, and when J cry out to you,
J hear your answer from your holy hill.
Psalm 3:3–4

Help me to reach out for you in times of need
knowing that you will be there for me.

———

O Beloved...
May I be dependable for me.
May I be dependable for all those I love.
May I be dependable for those in my community.
May I be dependable for those I struggle with or fear.
May I be dependable for all beings.

———

How do you show that you are dependable?

Strength

Al-Qawi

You, my Beloved, are my shepherd, I need
not long for anything; you create ease in my
life and replenish my inner strength. You
show me the still waters of my soul;
you renew my heart.

Psalm 23:1–3

Help me to draw upon your strength when I
feel my strength wavering.

———

O Beloved...

May I find renewed strength.
May all those I love find renewed strength.
May those in my community find renewed strength.
May those I struggle with or fear find renewed strength.
May all beings find renewed strength.

———

Where do you draw strength?

Steadfast
Al-Matin

Oh send out your steadfast light and your
forceful truth, my Beloved; let them lead me,
let them bring me to your holy hill
and into your heart.
Psalm 43:3

Help me to embrace the unwavering light of
truth that unites my body, mind, and soul,
and to extend that light to all.

———

O Beloved...
May I become steadfast in my truth.
May all those I love become steadfast in their truth.
May those in my community become
steadfast in their truth.
May those I struggle with or fear become
steadfast in their truth.
May all beings become steadfast in their truth.

———

How do you express steadfastness?

Deep Friendship
Al-Wali

For you, my Beloved, have been my hope, my trust, and my friend from my earliest days of youth. Upon you I have leaned from my birth, since the moment you embraced me and protected me in my mother's womb.

Psalm 71:5–6

Help me to celebrate and praise our deep friendship every day.

———•———

O Beloved…
May I experience deep friendships.
May all those I love experience deep friendships.
May those in my community experience deep friendships.
May those I struggle with or fear experience
deep friendships.
May all beings experience deep friendships.

———•———

How are you cultivating your
deep friendships?

Praiseworthy

Al-Hamid

J will sing to you, my Beloved, as long as J
live; J will sing praise to you while J have
being. May my meditation be pleasing to you,
for J rejoice in your love.

Psalm 104:33–34

Help me to discover what is praiseworthy in
me and in all who J meet, and to sing those
praises with gratitude daily.

O Beloved...

May I sing praises of gratitude for me.
May I sing praises of gratitude for all those I love.
May I sing praises of gratitude for those in my community.
May I sing praises of gratitude for
those I struggle with or fear.
May I sing praises of gratitude for all beings.

Who is in need of your praises today?

Accountability

Al-Mushi

For every beast of the forest is yours, my
Beloved, you appraise the cattle on a
thousand hills. You know all the birds of the
air, and all that moves in the field is yours.
Psalm 50:10–11

Help me to appreciate all of your creation and
to be accountable for my role in its care.

———

O Beloved…
May I be accountable to me.
May I be accountable to all those I love.
May I be accountable to those in my community.
May I be accountable to those I struggle with or fear.
May I be accountable to all beings.

———

What areas of your life would benefit from
greater accountability?

Original

Al-Mubdi

You brought me forth, my Beloved, from my
place of origin into the world; you delighted
in me because you formed me.

Psalm 18:19

Help me to perceive myself as the embodiment
of your original love and to share this
love with others.

O Beloved...

May I embody your original love.
May all those I love embody your original love.
May those in my community embody your original love.
May those I struggle with or fear embody
your original love.
May all beings embody your original love.

How are you offering your original love?

Restoration
Al-Muid

*Once you have spoken, my Beloved, and
twice have I heard this: that unconditional
love belongs to you; and with this love
you restore my heart.*
Psalm 62:11–12

Help me to fully receive your love for me and
to offer restoration to each heart I meet.

———

O Beloved...
May I enter into your restorative love.
May all those I love enter into your restorative love.
May those in my community enter into
your restorative love.
May those I struggle with or fear enter into
your restorative love.
May all beings enter into your restorative love.

———

How do you offer restoration?

Thriving
Al-Muhyi

I am thriving, my Beloved, for you have
given me life! I joyfully sing and make melody.
My soul has awakened, and with that I will
awake the world. I will give thanks to you
among all whom I meet; I will sing
praises to you everywhere.

Psalm 57:7–9

Help me to open my heart and to eagerly
express my joy each day.

———

O Beloved…
May I thrive.
May all those I love thrive.
May those in my community thrive.
May those I struggle with or fear thrive.
May all beings thrive.

———

In what areas of your life are you thriving?

Death

Al-Mumit

Even though I walk through the valley of the
shadow of death, I fear no harm; for you, my
Beloved, are with me at each step. Signs
of your presence comfort me.

Psalm 23:4

Help me to discover you everywhere, in light
and in shadow, in life and in death.

———•———

O Beloved...
May I find you in the shadows.
May all those I love find you in the shadows.
May those in my community find you in the shadows.
May those I struggle with or fear find you in the shadows.
May all beings find you in the shadows.

———•———

What shadows are troubling you?

Life Force
Al-Hayy

Dearly Beloved, your life force flows through everything. From your eternal abode you make springs gush forth in the valleys; they flow between the hills, they give drink to every beast of the field; the wild animals quench their thirst.
Psalm 104:10–11

Help me to recognize that you are the life force behind all and to celebrate the continual abundance of your blessings.

O Beloved…
May I embody my life force.
May all those I love embody their life force.
May those in my community embody their life force.
May those I struggle with or fear embody their life force.
May all beings embody their life force.

Where do you feel your life force?

Existence

Al-Qayyum

Yes, you light the lamp of all existence; my
Beloved, you lighten my darkness. You,
who need no light, are all light.

Psalm 18:28

Help me to comprehend your vast reach
touching all of existence and to nurture the
light-filled lamp within others and me.

———•———

O Beloved…
May I honor my existence.
May I honor the existence of all those I love.
May I honor the existence of those in my community.
May I honor the existence of those I struggle with or fear.
May I honor the existence of all beings.

———•———

Where do you touch existence?

Intuition
Al-Wajid

Dearly Beloved, let me intuit in the morning
your steadfast love, for in you I put my trust.
Teach me the way I should go,
as I lift up my soul to you.
Psalm 143:8

Help me to cultivate my path by tending and
listening to my intuition.

———

O Beloved...

May I trust the truth of my intuition.
May all those I love trust the truth of their intuition.
May those in my community trust the
truth of their intuition.
May those I struggle with or fear trust the
truth of their intuition.
May all beings trust the truth of their intuition.

———

How do you cultivate your intuition?

Illustrious

Al-Majid

I sing to you, my Beloved, with thanksgiving;
I make melody to your glorious nature upon
the lyre! You cover the heavens with clouds,
you prepare rain for the earth, you make
grass grow upon the hills—
all illustrious achievements.

Psalm 147:7–8

Help me to appreciate and celebrate the glory
of each moment and to see the beauty in
what I have to offer.

———

O Beloved...

May I appreciate and celebrate my illustrious nature.
May all those I love appreciate and celebrate
their illustrious nature.
May those in my community appreciate and celebrate
their illustrious nature.
May those I struggle with or fear appreciate and celebrate
their illustrious nature.
May all beings appreciate and celebrate
their illustrious nature.

———

How do you celebrate what is glorious?

Unity

Al-Wahid

Behold, my Beloved, how good and pleasant it
is when we all dwell in unity!
Psalm 133:1

Help me to embrace diversity while holding all
in the light of oneness.

———•———

O Beloved...
May I sense the unity of all.
May all those I love sense the unity of all.
May those in my community sense the unity of all.
May those I struggle with or fear sense the unity of all.
May all beings sense the unity of all.

———•———

Where can you create unity in your life?

Inclusion
Al-Ahad

Hear this, everyone, all are included! Listen
all inhabitants of the world, both low and high,
rich and poor together. My mouth speaks
wisdom; the meditation of my
heart is understanding.
Psalm 49:1–3

Help me to see the obvious,
that we are all one.

O Beloved…
May I feel included.
May all those I love feel included.
May those in my community feel included.
May those I struggle with or fear feel included.
May all beings feel included.

What efforts are involved to include people?

Refuge
As-Samad

I bless you, my Beloved, for the counsel you
provide; in the night, you instruct me through
my heart. I keep you always before me;
because having you near me provides refuge.
Therefore my heart is glad, and my soul
rejoices; my body also feels secure.

Psalm 16:7–9

Help me to trust that, through your refuge, all
is well and my needs will be satisfied.

———

O Beloved...
May I experience refuge in you.
May all those I love experience refuge in you.
May those in my community experience refuge in you.
May those I struggle with or fear experience refuge in you.
May all beings experience refuge in you.

———

Where might you find refuge?

Infinite Ability
Al-Qadir

Dearly Beloved, you are all powerful.
Behold, you are my helper; you have infinite
ability to uphold my life.
Psalm 54:4

Help me to recognize my many talents and to
apply them in the service of others.

———

O Beloved...
May I discover my infinite ability.
May all those I love discover their infinite ability.
May those in my community discover their infinite ability.
May those I struggle with or fear discover
their infinite ability.
May all beings discover their infinite ability.

———

What talents do you have to offer?

Power

Al-Muqtadir

Dearly Beloved, the creator of all power, your
voice is upon the waters; you of glory thunder
upon many seas. Your voice is powerful
and is full of majesty.

Psalm 29:3–4

Help me to fully realize my power and to
channel it appropriately in all situations.

———

O Beloved...

May I appropriately channel my power towards me.
May I appropriately channel my power towards
all those I love.
May I appropriately channel my power towards
those in my community.
May I appropriately channel my power towards
those I struggle with or fear.
May I appropriately channel my power towards all beings.

———

What is the appropriate use of power?

Acceleration
Al-Muqaddim

J sing praises to you, my Beloved, and give
thanks to your holy name. For your anger is
but for a moment, and your favor is for a
lifetime. Weeping may tarry for the night,
but you expedite the joy that comes
with the morning.
Psalm 30:4–5

Help me to be slow to anger and
to accelerate forgiveness.

———

O Beloved…

May I be quick to forgive me.
May I be quick to forgive all those I love.
May I be quick to forgive those in my community.
May I be quick to forgive those I struggle with or fear.
May I be quick to forgive all beings.

———

How would you benefit from accelerating
your ability to forgive?

Regressing
Al-Muakhkhir

Dearly Beloved, I am regressing. You
know my folly; the struggles I have
are not hidden from you.
Psalm 69:5

Help me to be patient when I feel a delay
in the unfolding of full consciousness
in myself or others.

———•———

O Beloved...
May I transform my regressions.
May all those I love transform their regressions.
May those in my community transform their regressions.
May those I struggle with or fear transform
their regressions.
May all beings transform their regressions.

———•———

In what areas of your life are you
experiencing regression?

Alpha
Al-Awwal

Dearly Beloved, you begin each morning
drenching me with your unconditional love;
I rejoice and am glad all of my days.
Psalm 90:14

Help me to embrace your love as my first
light today and always.

———

O Beloved…
May I embrace me with first light.
May I embrace all those I love with first light.
May I embrace those in my community with first light.
May I embrace those I struggle with or fear with first light.
May I embrace all beings with first light.

———

How do you first enter your day?

Omega

Al-Akhir

May you live while the sun lasts, my Beloved,
and as long as the moon, throughout all
generations, up to the very end. May you be
like rain that falls on the mown grass, like
showers that water the earth!
In your days may righteousness flourish,
and peace abound, until Omega.

Psalm 72:5–7

Help me to comprehend your vast, lasting
presence, and to provide replenishing peace
to me and those I encounter.

———

O Beloved…

May I be a lasting presence for me.
May I be a lasting presence for all those I love.
May I be a lasting presence for those in my community.
May I be a lasting presence for those I struggle with or fear.
May I be a lasting presence for all beings.

———

Who might you be a lasting
presence for today?

Manifesting
Az-Zahir

Dearly Beloved, you reveal clearly my light
and my truth; in this you manifest safety. You
are the foundation of my life; there is
no need for me to be afraid.
Psalm 27:1

Help me to sense your presence
in all circumstances.

———

O Beloved...
May I manifest light and truth.
May all those I love manifest light and truth.
May those in my community manifest light and truth.
May those I struggle with or fear manifest light and truth.
May all beings manifest light and truth.

———

What in your life is asking to be manifested?

Hidden

Al-Batin

J sink in deep mire, where there is no foothold;
my Beloved, J have come into deep waters,
and the flood sweeps over me. J am weary
with my crying; my throat is parched.
You are hidden from me. My eyes
grow dim as J wait for you.

Psalm 69:2–3

Help me to trust that you are still with me when
J cannot find your light and to search inside
myself for your presence.

―――

O Beloved...

May I discover you hidden within me.
May all those I love discover you hidden within.
May those in my community discover you hidden within.
May those I struggle with or fear discover
you hidden within.
May all beings discover you hidden within.

―――

What is hidden within you?

Governing

Al-Wali

Dearly Beloved, you govern and guide me.
You guard my coming and going,
now and always.
Psalm 121:8

Help me to feel your hand leading me to what
is best for me and to let go of that which no
longer serves me.

———

O Beloved...
May I feel your governing presence.
May all those I love feel your governing presence.
May those in my community feel your governing presence.
May those I struggle with or fear feel
your governing presence.
May all beings feel your governing presence.

———

What area of your life is in need of governing?

Utmost

Al-Muta ali

Dearly Beloved, I trust in you, and live my life
accordingly so that I can feel the security you
offer. I take delight in you, and you provide
me the utmost desires of my heart. I commit
my way to your supreme ways;
I trust in you and you act.

Psalm 37:3–5

Help me to fulfill my desires according
to your truth.

———

O Beloved...
May I desire truth.
May all those I love desire truth.
May those in my community desire truth.
May those I struggle with or fear desire truth.
May all beings desire truth.

———

What is most needed in your life right now?

Kindness

Al-Barr

Gracious is my Beloved, and kind and merciful. You preserve the simple; when I was brought low, you saved me. My soul rests in your kindness; for you are generous with me. You have delivered my soul from heartache, my eyes from tears, my feet from stumbling.

Psalm 116:5–9

Help me to walk with you in kindness and compassion and to extend this gift to others.

———

O Beloved…

May I walk in your kindness.
May all those I love walk in your kindness.
May those in my community walk in your kindness.
May those I struggle with or fear walk in your kindness.
May all beings walk in your kindness.

———

Who is in need of your kindness?

Restoring Equilibrium
At-Tawwab

Restore my equilibrium with your joy, my
Beloved, and uphold me with a
balanced and willing spirit.
Psalm 51:12

Help me to center myself as I both embrace
and release the complexities of life.

O Beloved…

May I be restored to equilibrium.
May all those I love be restored to equilibrium.
May those in my community be restored to equilibrium.
May those I struggle with or fear
be restored to equilibrium.
May all beings be restored to equilibrium.

What might you do to restore balance
for yourself?

Falling
Al-Muntaqim

Dearly Beloved, all my longing is known to you, my sighing is not hidden from you. My heart throbs, my strength fails me; and the light of my eyes—it also has gone from me. I am falling.
Psalm 38:9–10

Help me to hold on to you as I descend under the gravity of my suffering and to shower others and me with compassion.

O Beloved...
May I find you when I am falling.
May all those I love find you when they are falling.
May those in my community find you when they are falling.
May those I struggle with or fear
find you when they are falling.
May all beings find you when they are falling.

What do you do when you are falling?

Pardoning

Al-Afuww

J am mindful of your mercy and of your
pardoning ways, for they have existed from
the beginning. Remember not my
transgressions, my Beloved; in your
forgiveness, remember me.
Psalm 25:6–7

Help me to not take things personally, to
forgive myself, and to easily pardon others
for any perceived slights.

———

O Beloved...
May I be quick to pardon me.
May I be quick to pardon all those I love.
May I be quick to pardon those in my community.
May I be quick to pardon those I struggle with or fear.
May I be quick to pardon all beings.

———

What areas of your life are in need
of pardoning?

Healing
Ar-Rauf

Be gracious to me, my Beloved, for I am
languishing; heal me, for my body and mind
are troubled. My soul also is suffering. In
your clemently ways, make me whole in
your steadfast love.

Psalm 6:2–4

Help me to embody all that is healthy for me,
to let go of that which is not, and to spread
healing through thoughts, words,
and deeds to all.

———

O Beloved…
May I embody healing.
May all those I love embody healing.
May those in my community embody healing.
May those I struggle with or fear embody healing.
May all beings embody healing.

———

What within you needs healing?

Interconnection
Malik-ul-Mulk

Connect with me, my Beloved, for in my
relationship with you I find peace. I say to
you, "You own everything, it is all of you;
apart from you I am confused."
Psalm 16:1–2

Help me to delight in the deep interconnections
that I make with those whom you
place in my path.

———

O Beloved…
May I feel deeply interconnected to you.
May all those I love feel deeply interconnected to you.
May those in my community feel deeply
interconnected to you.
May those I struggle with or fear feel deeply
interconnected to you.
May all beings feel deeply interconnected to you.

———

With whom are your deepest connections?

Bounty

Dhu-l-Jalali wa-l-ikram

J look to thee, my Beloved, to give me bounty
in due season. When you give to me, J gather
it up; when you open your hand, J am filled
with good things. When J cannot find you, J
miss you; when J die, J will return to dust and
renew the majestic ground with my spirit.
Psalm 104:27–30

Help me to receive your bounty, delight in your
majesty, and offer my own bounty to others.

———

O Beloved...
May I delight in your bounty.
May all those I love delight in your bounty.
May those in my community delight in your bounty.
May those I struggle with or fear delight in your bounty.
May all beings delight in your bounty.

———

What bounty do you have to share?

Equanimity

Al-Muqsit

Let the words of my mouth and the meditation
of my heart create equanimity, my Beloved,
and be acceptable in your sight,
you who are equitable to all.
Psalm 19:14

Help me to foster serenity and calm in my mind
and heart, and to invite equanimity
into all circumstances.

———

O Beloved...
May I experience equanimity.
May all those I love experience equanimity.
May those in my community experience equanimity.
May those I struggle with or fear experience equanimity.
May all beings experience equanimity.

———

How do you foster equanimity?

Gather

Al-Jami

Honor and majesty are before you, my
Beloved; you gather strength and beauty
into your sanctuary.
Psalm 96:6

Help me to lay bare the holy place within me
and to receive and give thanks for all that you
gather and bestow upon me.

———

O Beloved...
May I gather in your sanctuary.
May all those I love gather in your sanctuary.
May those in my community gather in your sanctuary.
May those I struggle with or fear gather in your sanctuary.
May all beings gather in your sanctuary.

———

Who would you like to gather towards you?

Abundance
Al-Ghani

But I will hope continually, and will praise
you, my Beloved, yet more and more. My
mouth will tell of your richness, of your deeds
of abundance all the day, for their number
is past my knowledge.

Psalm 71:14–15

Help me to relinquish scarcity thinking and to
relish the abundance in all that you provide.

———

O Beloved...
May I experience abundance.
May all those I love experience abundance.
May those in my community experience abundance.
May those I struggle with or fear experience abundance.
May all beings experience abundance.

———

Where is abundance flowing in your life?

Enrichment
Al-Mughni

You, my Beloved, visited the earth and
watered it, you greatly enriched it; the river
of love is full of water; you provided my grain,
and prepared all that I needed.
Psalm 65:9

Help me to see clearly how you enrich my
life with your love each day.

———

O Beloved...
May I be enriched by your divine love.
May all those I love be enriched by your divine love.
May those in my community be enriched
by your divine love.
May those I struggle with or fear be enriched
by your divine love.
May all beings be enriched by your divine love.

———

What enriches your life?

Prevention

Al-Mani

You are a stronghold for the oppressed, my Beloved, a stronghold in times of trouble. My trust in you prevents my struggles from overwhelming me.

Psalm 9:9–10

Help me to maintain perspective of my challenges by stilling my mind when it is racing and churning.

———•———

O Beloved…
May I learn to still my mind.
May all those I love learn to still their mind.
May those in my community learn to still their mind.
May those I struggle with or fear learn to still their mind.
May all beings learn to still their mind.

———•———

What skills do you draw upon to maintain perspective?

Pain and Loss

Al-Darr

Turn to me, my Beloved, and pour down your
mercy and compassion on me; for I am lonely
and afflicted. Relieve the troubles of my heart,
and bring me out of my distresses. Consider
my pain and my loss, and create
ease in my journey.
Psalm 25:16–18

Help me to move through suffering with
steadiness and to know that you are holding
me at every step.

———

O Beloved...
May I feel held by you.
May all those I love feel held by you.
May those in my community feel held by you.
May those I struggle with or fear feel held by you.
May all beings feel held by you.

———

What might help relieve your suffering?

Goodness

An-Nafi

You have multiplied, my Beloved, your
wondrous deeds and your good thoughts
toward us; none can compare with your
goodness! Were I to proclaim and tell of them,
your good deeds would be more
than can be numbered.

Psalm 40:5

Help me to experience the goodness that
fills my heart and surrounds me and to be
intentional in my thoughts, words, and deeds.

———

O Beloved...

May I share my innate goodness.
May all those I love share their innate goodness.
May those in my community share their innate goodness.
May those I struggle with or fear share
their innate goodness.
May all beings share their innate goodness.

———

Where do you recognize goodness?

Light
An-Nur

How precious is your unconditional love, my
Beloved, in the shadow of your wings we find
a sanctuary. I feast abundantly and drink
from the river of your delights. You are the
fountain of life; in your light do I find light.

Psalm 36:7–9

Help me to express the light that resides
in me with the world.

———

O Beloved...
May I express my light with me.
May I express my light with all those I love.
May I express my light with those in my community.
May I express my light with those I struggle with or fear.
May I express my light with all beings.

———

How do you share your light?

Guidance
Al-Hadi

Yea, you are my rock and my fortress; dearly
Beloved, lead me and guide me safely into
everything that life requires of me, for you are
my refuge. Into your hand I commit my spirit;
your faithful guidance has restored me.
Psalm 31:3–5

Help me to recognize and follow your
guidance in each moment.

———•———

O Beloved...
May I follow your guidance.
May all those I love follow your guidance.
May those in my community follow your guidance.
May those I struggle with or fear follow your guidance.
May all beings follow your guidance.

———•———

What areas of your life are in
need of guidance?

Invitation

Al-Badi

I hear your invitation, my Beloved, the
wonder that each heart has heard and known,
that ancestors revealed; your original and
unconditional love for me and all that
you have created.
Psalm 78:1–3

Help me to be an invitation into love and to
celebrate with gratitude all that you have
revealed to me.

———

O Beloved...

May I be an invitation of love to me.
May I be an invitation of love to all those I love.
May I be an invitation of love to those in my community.
May I be an invitation of love to those
I struggle with or fear.
May I be an invitation of love to all beings.

———

How will you be an invitation today?

Endurance
Al-Baqi

You, my Beloved, are near to the
brokenhearted, and you provide endurance
to all who are crushed in spirit.
Psalm 34:18

Help me to embody your everlasting strength
and endurance especially in times of despair.

———•———

O Beloved…
May I develop endurance.
May all those I love develop endurance.
May those in my community develop endurance.
May those I struggle with or fear develop endurance.
May all beings develop endurance.

———•———

How do you cultivate endurance?

Ownership
Al-Warith

You direct me to diligently follow your precepts, my Beloved, and to honor all that you own, all that is yours. O that my ways may be unwavering in keeping your statutes!
Psalm 119:4–5

Help me to embrace the inheritance of your divine grace and, with your guidance, to return once again to your path of truth.

———

O Beloved...
May I own my path of truth.
May all those I love own their path of truth.
May those in my community own their path of truth.
May those I struggle with or fear own their path of truth.
May all beings own their path of truth.

———

For what do you need to take ownership?

Teach

Ar-Rashid

Teach me your way, my Beloved, that J may walk in your truth; unite my heart to embrace your name. J give thanks to you with my whole heart, and J will glorify you forever.

Psalm 86:11–12

Help me to follow your wisdom so that J may be a teacher of love to all.

———

O Beloved...

May I embrace my inner teacher.
May all those I love embrace their inner teacher.
May those in my community embrace their inner teacher.
May those I struggle with or fear embrace
their inner teacher.
May all beings embrace their inner teacher.

———

What is your inner teacher telling you?

Patience

As-Sabur

I believe that I shall see the goodness of you,
my Beloved, in all who I encounter. In my
patience, I wait for this goodness to be
revealed; I am strong, and my heart takes
courage; yes, I wait for you to be
unveiled in all!
Psalm 27:13–14

Help me, when I cannot find you, to be patient
and trust that you are present.

———

O Beloved…

May I embody patience and trust.
May all those I love embody patience and trust.
May those in my community embody patience and trust.
May those I struggle with or fear embody
patience and trust.
May all beings embody patience and trust.

———

How do you cultivate patience?

Moving Forward in an Interfaith World

Less Judgment, More Curiosity

A few months ago I saw a bumper sticker that said: "Less Judgment, More Curiosity." This phrase stopped me short. I have been thinking about it ever since, especially as it relates to living in a multi-faith world. Every aspect of interfaith that I have experienced has required less judgment and more curiosity on my part. This is true whether I am referring to being of service or allowing my interfaith experience to transform me. The following are a few examples of what engaging in interfaith appreciation and cooperation has taught me about judgment and curiosity.

Engaging in an interfaith world invites us to be curious about our commonalities *and* to have less judgment about our differences. It encourages us to deepen into our own faith and practices *and* to learn more about other beliefs and customs. It requires us to acknowledge the limitations of our own doctrines *and* to respect the doctrines of all faiths.

Engaging in an interfaith world invites us to suspend value judgments of what is not known *and* opens us to embrace the delight of discovering what is not yet known. It asks us to acknowledge our discomfort with the unfamiliar *and* expand our thinking beyond this uneasiness. It encourages us recognize that our "expertise" can create impenetrable walls *and* that these walls dissolve when we relax into "beginner's mind." It requires us to look square in the face of our prejudices *and* to forgive others and ourselves for the messy human beings that we are.

Engaging in an interfaith world disposes us to investigate our fears *and* move through those fears. It asks us to examine issues such as scarcity thinking (this is mine and there is only enough for me) *and* moves us towards abundance thinking (this is mine and there will be enough if all share what they have). It encourages us to acknowledge the intolerance that is rife in our society *and* teaches us how to embrace those who are different from us. It requires us to be present in the world, enter it from a place of love, *and* make a difference…one person, one community, one neighborhood at a time.

What have you discovered engaging in an interfaith world? How has this influenced your awareness of your own judgment and curiosity? How will this lead you to embrace the Beloved and cultivate compassion?

Select Qur'an Verses for the Ninety-Nine Names of God

—The Holy Qur'an, translated by M. H. Shakir and published by Tahrike Tarsile Qur'an, Inc., in 1983.

Ar-Rahman, The Most Compassionate

And your God is one God! there is no god but He; He is the Compassionate, the Merciful. —Qur'an, 2.163

Ar-Rahim, The All Merciful

Lord! we believe, so do Thou forgive us and have mercy on us, and Thou art the best of the Merciful ones.

—Qur'an, 23.109

Al-Malik, The Sovereign

Therefore glory be to Him in Whose hand is the kingdom of all things, and to Him you shall be brought back.

—Qur'an, 36.83

Al-Quddus, The Pure One

Whatever is in the heavens and whatever is in the earth declares the glory of Allah, the King, the Holy, the Mighty, the Wise. —Qur'an, 62.1

As-Salaam, The Source of Peace

And Allah invites to the abode of peace and guides whom He pleases into the right path. —Qur'an, 10.25

Al-Mumin, The Inspirer of Faith

Allah will most certainly establish for them their religion which He has chosen for them, and that He will most certainly, after their fear, give them security in exchange.

—Qur'an, 24.55

Al-Muhaymin, The Guardian

Surely I rely on Allah, my Lord and your Lord; there is no living creature but He holds it by its forelock. —Qur'an, 11.56

Al-Aziz, The Victorious

Enter upon them by the gate, for when you have entered it you shall surely be victorious, and on Allah should you rely if you are believers. —Qur'an, 5.23

Al-Jabbar, The Compeller

And you do not will, except as Allah wills. —Qur'an, 76.30

Al-Mutakabbir, The Greatest

And to Him belongs greatness in the heavens and the earth.
—Qur'an, 45.37

Al-Khaliq, The Creator

Is not He Who created the heavens and the earth able to create the like of them? Yea! and He is the Creator (of all), the Knower. —Qur'an, 36.81

Al-Bari, The Maker of Order

Who made good everything that He has created, and He began the creation of man from dust. —Qur'an, 32.7

Al-Musawwir, The Shaper of Beauty

He formed you, then made goodly your forms, and He provided you with goodly things; that is Allah, your Lord; blessed then is Allah, the Lord of the worlds. —Qur'an, 40.64

Al-Ghaffar, The Forgiving

And most surely I am most Forgiving to him who repents and believes and does good, then continues to follow the right direction. —Qur'an, 20.82

Al-Qahhar, The Crusher

And to Him submits whoever is in the heavens and the earth, willingly or unwillingly, and to Him shall they be returned.

—Qur'an, 3.83

Al-Wahhab, The Giver of All

Say: Surely grace is in the hand of Allah, He gives it to whom He pleases; and Allah is Ample-giving, Knowing.

—Qur'an, 3.73

Ar-Razzaq, The Sustainer

And how many a living creature that does not carry its sustenance: Allah sustains it and yourselves. —Qur'an, 29.60

Al-Fattah, The Opener

Therefore (for) whomsoever Allah intends that He would guide him aright, He expands his breast for Islam.

—Qur'an, 6.125

Al-Alim, The Knower of All

And know that Allah knows what is in your minds.

—Qur'an, 2.235

Al-Qabid, The Constrictor

Allah takes the souls at the time of their death, and those that die not during their sleep; then He withholds those on whom He has passed the decree of death and sends the others back till an appointed term. —Qur'an, 39.42

Al-Basit, The Reliever

Allah amplifies and straitens the means of subsistence for whom He pleases; and they rejoice in this world's life.

—Qur'an, 13.26

Al-Khafid, The Abaser

By the soul and Him Who made it perfect; then He inspired it to understand what is right and wrong for it.

—Qur'an, 91.7–8

Ar-Rafi, The Exalter

Allah will exalt those of you who believe, and those who are given knowledge, in high degrees. —Qur'an, 58.11

Al-Muizz, The Bestower of Honor

Thou exaltest whom Thou pleasest and abasest whom Thou pleasest; in Thine hand is the good. —Qur'an, 3.26

Al-Mudhill, The Humiliator

Surely the disgrace and the evil are this day upon the unbelievers. —Qur'an, 16.27

As-Sami, The Hearer of All

He said: Fear not, surely I am with you both: I do hear and see. —Qur'an, 20.46

Al-Basir, The Seer of All

So you shall remember what I say to you, and I entrust my affair to Allah, Surely Allah sees the servants. —Qur'an, 40.44

Al-Hakam, The Judge

And call not with Allah any other god; there is no god but He, every thing is perishable but He; His is the judgment, and to Him you shall be brought back. —Qur'an, 28.88

Al-Adl, The Just

And We will set up a just balance on the day of resurrection, so no soul shall be dealt with unjustly in the least; and though there be the weight of a grain of mustard seed, (yet) will We bring it, and sufficient are We to take account.

—Qur'an, 21.47

Al-Latif, The Subtle One

Vision comprehends Him not, and He comprehends (all) vision; and He is the Knower of subtleties, the Aware.

—Qur'an, 6.103

Al-Khabir, The All Aware

Surely He is Cognizant of what is in the hearts. Does He not know, Who created? And He is the Knower of the subtleties, the Aware. —Qur'an, 67.13–14

Al-Halim, The Forbearing

And whatever affliction befalls you, it is on account of what your hands have wrought, and (yet) He pardons most (of your faults). —Qur'an, 42.30

Al-Azim, The Magnificent

His knowledge extends over the heavens and the earth, and the preservation of them both tires Him not, and He is the Most High, the Magnificent —Qur'an, 2.255

Al-Ghafur, The Hider of Faults

Inform My servants that I am the Forgiving, the Merciful.

—Qur'an, 15.49

Ash-Shakur, The Rewarder of Thankfulness

And when your Lord made it known: If you are grateful, I would certainly give to you more. —Qur'an, 14.7

Al-Ali, The Highest

Possessor of the highest rank, Lord of power: He makes the inspiration to light by His command upon whom He pleases of His servants. —Qur'an, 40.15

Al-Kabir, The Greatest

He is Allah...the Possessor of every greatness. Glory be to Allah from what they set up (with Him). —Qur'an, 59.23

Al-Hafiz, The Preserver

Surely my Lord is the Preserver of all things. —Qur'an, 11.57

Al-Muqit, The Nourisher

And there is no animal in the earth but on Allah is the sustenance of it. —Qur'an, 11.6

Al-Hasib, The Accounter

Those who deliver the messages of Allah and fear Him, and do not fear any one but Allah; and Allah is sufficient to take account. —Qur'an, 33.39

Al-Jalil, The Mighty

Allah bears witness that there is no god but He, and (so do) the angels and those possessed of knowledge, maintaining His creation with justice; there is no god but He, the Mighty, the Wise. —Qur'an, 3.18

Al-Karim, The Generous

Who is it that will offer of Allah a goodly gift, so He will multiply it to him manifold, and Allah straitens and amplifies, and you shall be returned to Him. —Qur'an, 2.245

Ar-Raqib, The Watchful One

He knows that which goes deep down into the earth and that which comes forth out of it, and that which comes down from the heaven and that which goes up into it, and He is with you wherever you are; and Allah sees what you do.

—Qur'an, 57.4

Al-Mujib, The Responder to Prayer

Who answers the distressed one when he calls upon Him and removes the evil, and He will make you successors in the earth. —Qur'an, 27.62

Al-Wasi, The All Comprehending

If the sea were ink for the words of my Lord, the sea would surely be consumed before the words of my Lord are exhausted. —Qur'an, 18.109

Al-Hakim, The Perfectly Wise

He grants wisdom to whom He pleases, and whoever is granted wisdom, he indeed is given a great good and none but men of understanding mind. —Qur'an, 2.269

Al-Wadud, The Loving One

If you love Allah, then follow me, Allah will love you and forgive you your faults. —Qur'an, 3.31

Al-Majid, The Majestic One

The mercy of Allah and His blessings are on you, O people of the house, surely He is Praised, Glorious. —Qur'an, 11.73

Al-Baith, The Resurrector

And they say: What! when we shall have become bones and decayed particles, shall we then certainly be raised up, being a new creation? —Qur'an, 17.49

Ash-Shahid, The Witness

Whose is the kingdom of the heavens and the earth; and Allah is a Witness of all things. —Qur'an, 85.9

Al-Haqq, The Truth

This is because Allah is the Truth, and that which they call upon besides Him is the falsehood. —Qur'an, 31.30

Al-Wakil, The Trustee

So when you have decided, then place your trust in Allah; surely Allah loves those who trust. —Qur'an, 3.159

Al-Qawi, The Possessor of All Strength

Who is mightier in strength than we? Did they not see that Allah Who created them was mightier than they in strength?
—Qur'an, 41.15

Al-Matin, The Forceful One

And the thunder declares His glory with His praise, and the angels too for awe of Him; and He sends the thunderbolts and smites with them whom He pleases, yet they dispute concerning Allah, and He is mighty in prowess. —Qur'an, 13.13

Al-Wali, The Friend and Protector

And whatever is in the heavens and whatever is in the earth is Allah's, and Allah is sufficient as a Protector. —Qur'an, 4.132

Al-Hamid, The Praised One

The seven heavens declare His glory and the earth (too), and those who are in them; and there is not a single thing but glorifies Him with His praise. —Qur'an, 17.44

Al-Mushi, The Appraiser

What a book is this! it does not omit a small one nor a great one, but numbers them (all); and what they had done they shall find present (there). —Qur'an, 18.49

Al-Mubdi, The Originator

Allah originates the creation, then reproduces it, then to Him you shall be brought back. —Qur'an, 30.11

Al-Muid, The Restorer

And when I am sick, then He restores me to health.

—Qur'an, 26.80

Al-Muhyi, The Giver of Life

And He it is Who has brought you to life, then He will cause you to die, then bring you to life (again). —Qur'an, 22.66

Al-Mumit, The Taker of Life

Surely We give life and cause to die, and to Us is the eventual coming. —Qur'an, 50.43

Al-Hayy, The Everliving One

Allah, (there is) no god but He, the Everliving, the Self-subsisting by Whom all things subsist. —Qur'an, 3.2

Al-Qayyum, The Self-Existing One

And certainly We created the heavens and the earth and what is between them in six periods and there touched Us not any fatigue. —Qur'an, 50.38

Al-Wajid, The Finder

Did He not find you an orphan and give you shelter? And find you lost (unrecognized by men) and guide (them to you)? And find you in want and make you to be free from want? —Qur'an, 93.6–8

Al-Majid, The Glorious

Do you wonder at Allah's bidding? The mercy of Allah and His blessings are on you, O people of the house, surely He is Praised, Glorious. —Qur'an, 11.73

Al-Wahid, The Only One

Say: He, Allah, is One. Allah is He on Whom all depend. He begets not, nor is He begotten. And none is like Him.

—Qur'an, 112.1–4

Al-Ahad, The One

So your God is One God, therefore to Him should you submit, and give good news to the humble. —Qur'an, 22.34

As-Samad, The Satsifier of Needs

I seek Allah's refuge, surely my Lord made good my abode: Surely the unjust do not prosper. —Qur'an, 12.23

Al-Qadir, The All Powerful

Allah creates what He pleases; surely Allah has power over all things. —Qur'an, 24.45

Al-Muqtadir, The Creator of Power

Surely those who guard (against evil) shall be in gardens and rivers, In the seat of honor with a most Powerful King.

—Qur'an, 54.54–55

Al-Muqaddim, The Expediter

And the foremost are the foremost, These are they who are drawn nigh (to Allah), In the gardens of bliss.

—Qur'an, 56.10–12

Al-Muakhkhir, The Delayer

You have the appointment of a day from which you cannot hold back any while, nor can you bring it on. —Qur'an, 34.30

Al-Awwal, The First

He is the First and the Last and the Ascendant (over all) and the Knower of hidden things, and He is Cognizant of all things. —Qur'an, 57.3

Al-Akhir, The Last

Say: The first and the last, shall most surely be gathered together for the appointed hour of a known day.

—Qur'an, 56.49

Az-Zahir, The Manifest One

He it is Who sent His Apostle with guidance and the religion of truth, that He might cause it to prevail over all religions.

—Qur'an, 9.33

Al-Batin, The Hidden One

O our Lord! Surely Thou knowest what we hide and what we make public, and nothing in the earth nor any thing in heaven is hidden from Allah. —Qur'an, 14.38

Al-Wali, The Governor

For his sake there are angels following one another, before him and behind him, who guard him by Allah's commandment; surely Allah does not change the condition of a people until they change their own condition. —Qur'an, 13.11

Al-Muta ali, The Supreme One

And that do not exalt yourselves against Allah, surely I will bring to you a clear authority. —Qur'an, 44.19

Al-Barr, The Doer of God

These are they from whom We accept the best of what they have done and pass over their evil deeds, among the dwellers of the garden; the promise of truth which they were promised. —Qur'an, 46.16

At-Tawwab, The Guide to Repentance

And He it is Who accepts repentance from His servants and pardons the evil deeds and He knows what you do.

—Qur'an, 42.25

Al-Muntaqim, The Avenger

To whomsoever My wrath is due shall perish indeed.

—Qur'an, 20.81

Al-Afuww, The Forgiver

Most surely Allah is Pardoning, Forgiving. —Qur'an, 22.60

Ar-Rauf, The Clement

Allah desires that He should make light your burdens, and man is created weak. —Qur'an, 4.28

Malik-ul-Mulk, The Owner of All

And whoever is in the heavens and the earth makes obeisance to Allah only, willingly and unwillingly, and their shadows too at morn and eve. —Qur'an, 13.15

Dhu-l-Jalali wa-l-ikram, The Lord of Majesty and Bounty

O you who believe! bow down and prostrate yourselves and serve your Lord, and do good that you may succeed.

—Qur'an, 22.77

Al-Muqsit, The Equitable One

Say: My Lord has enjoined justice, and set upright your faces at every time of prayer and call on Him, being sincere to Him in obedience; as He brought you forth in the beginning, so shall you also return. —Qur'an, 7.29

Al-Jami, The Gatherer

Our Lord! surely Thou art the Gatherer of men on a day about which there is no doubt; surely Allah will not fail (His) promise. —Qur'an, 3.9

Al-Ghani, The Rich One

And whoever strives hard, he strives only for his own soul; most surely Allah is Self-sufficient, above (need of) the worlds.
—Qur'an, 29.6

Al-Mughni, The Enricher

And that He it is Who enriches and gives to hold.
—Qur'an, 53.48

Al-Mani, The Preventor of Harm

They shall not harm you in any way, and Allah has revealed to you the Book and the wisdom, and He has taught you what you did not know, and Allah's grace on you is very great.
—Qur'an, 4.113

Al-Darr, The Creator of Harm

And if Allah touches you with affliction, there is none to take it off but He; and if He visits you with good, then He has power over all things. —Qur'an, 6.17

An-Nafi, The Creator of Good

Who created me, then He has shown me the way: And He Who gives me to eat and gives me to drink: And when I am sick, then He restores me to health. —Qur'an, 26.78–80

An-Nur, The Light

Therefore believe in Allah and His Apostle and the Light which We have revealed. —Qur'an, 64.8

Al-Hadi, The Guide

Surely (as for) those who believe and do good, their Lord will guide them by their faith; there shall flow from beneath them rivers in gardens of bliss. —Qur'an, 10.9

Al-Badi, The Originator

Wonderful Originator of the heavens and the earth, and when He decrees an affair, He only says to it, Be, so there it is. —Qur'an, 2.117

Al-Baqi, The Everlasting One

And call not with Allah any other god; there is no god but He, every thing is perishable but He. —Qur'an, 28.88

Al-Warith, The Inheritor of All

Ask help from Allah and be patient; surely the land is Allah's; He causes such of His servants to inherit it as He pleases, and the end is for those who guard (against evil). —Qur'an, 7.128

Ar-Rashid, The Righteous Teacher

Allah teaches you, and Allah knows all things. —Qur'an, 2.282

As-Sabur, The Patient One

O you who believe! seek assistance through patience and prayer; surely Allah is with the patient. —Qur'an, 2.153

Original Psalm Verses Selected for the 99 Meditations

—Revised Standard Version Bible, Second Catholic Edition (2009). Ft. Collins, CO: Ignatius Press.

Psalm 3:3–4

But thou, O LORD, art a shield about me, my glory, and the lifter of my head. I cry aloud to the LORD, and he answers me from his holy hill.

Psalm 3:5

I lie down and sleep; I wake again, for the LORD sustains me.

Psalm 4:8

In peace I will both lie down and sleep; for thou alone, O Lord, makest me dwell in safety.

Psalm 6:2–4

Be gracious to me, O LORD, for I am languishing; O LORD, heal me, for my bones are troubled. My soul also is sorely troubled. But thou, O LORD—how long? Turn, O LORD, save my life; deliver me for the sake of thy steadfast love.

Psalm 8:3–4

When I look at thy heavens, the work of thy fingers, the moon and the stars which thou hast established; what is man that thou art mindful of him, and the son of man that thou dost care for him?

Psalm 9:1–2

I will give thanks to the Lord with my whole heart; I will tell of all thy wonderful deeds. I will be glad and exult in thee, I will sing praise to thy name, O Most High.

Psalm 9:9–10

The LORD is a stronghold for the oppressed, a stronghold in times of trouble. And those who know thy name put their trust in thee, for thou, O LORD, hast not forsaken those who seek thee.

Psalm 13:5–6

But I have trusted in thy steadfast love; my heart shall rejoice in thy salvation. I will sing to the LORD, because he has dealt bountifully with me.

Psalm 16:1–2

Preserve me, O God, for in thee I take refuge. I say to the LORD, "Thou art my Lord; I have no good apart from thee."

Psalm 16:7–9

I bless the LORD who gives me counsel; in the night also my heart instructs me. I keep the LORD always before me; because he is at my right hand, I shall not be moved. Therefore my heart is glad, and my soul rejoices; my body also dwells secure.

Psalm 16:11

Thou dost show me the path of life; in thy presence there is fullness of joy, in thy right hand are pleasures for evermore.

Psalm 17:5–7

My steps have held fast to thy paths, my feet have not slipped. I call upon thee, for thou wilt answer me, O God; incline thy ear to me, hear my words. Wondrously show thy steadfast love, O savior of those who seek refuge from their adversaries at thy right hand.

Psalm 18:19

He brought me forth into a broad place; he delivered me, because he delighted in me.

Psalm 18:28

Yea, thou dost light my lamp; the LORD my God lightens my darkness.

Psalm 19:1–4

The heavens are telling the glory of God; and the firmament proclaims his handiwork. Day to day pours forth speech, and night to night declares knowledge. There is no speech, nor are there words; their voice is not heard; yet their voice goes out through all the earth, and their words to the end of the world.

Psalm 19:7–9

The law of the LORD is perfect, reviving the soul; the testimony of the LORD is sure, making wise the simple; the precepts of the LORD are right, rejoicing the heart; the commandment of the LORD is pure, enlightening the eyes; the fear of the LORD is clean, enduring forever; the ordinances of the LORD are true, and righteous altogether.

Psalm 19:14

Let the words of my mouth and the meditation of my heart be acceptable in thy sight, O LORD, my rock and my redeemer.

Psalm 20:4

May he grant you your heart's desire, and fulfill all your plans!

Psalm 23:1–3

The Lord is my shepherd, I shall not want; he makes me lie down in green pastures. He leads me beside still waters; he restores my soul.

Psalm 23:4

Even though I walk through the valley of the shadow of death, I fear no evil; for thou art with me; thy rod and thy staff, they comfort me.

Psalm 25:4–5

Make me to know thy ways, O LORD; teach me thy paths. Lead me in thy truth, and teach me, for thou art the God of my salvation; for thee I wait all the day long.

Psalm 25:6–7

Be mindful of thy mercy, O LORD, and of thy steadfast love, for they have been from of old. Remember not the sins of my youth, or my transgressions; according to thy steadfast love remember me, for thy goodness' sake, O LORD!

Psalm 25:16–18

Turn thou to me, and be gracious to me; for I am lonely and afflicted. Relieve the troubles of my heart, and bring me out of my distresses. Consider my affliction and my trouble, and forgive all my sins.

Psalm 27:1

The LORD is my light and my salvation; whom shall I fear? The LORD is the stronghold of my life; of whom shall I be afraid?

Psalm 27:4–5

One thing have I asked of the LORD, that will I seek after; that I may dwell in the house of the LORD all the days of my life, to behold the beauty of the LORD, and to inquire in his temple. For he will hide me in his shelter in the day of trouble; he will conceal me under the cover of his tent, he will set me high upon a rock.

Psalm 27:7–8

Hear, O LORD, when I cry aloud, be gracious to me and answer me! Thou hast said, "Seek ye my face." My heart says to thee, "Thy face, LORD, do I seek."

Psalm 27:13–14

I believe that I shall see the goodness of the LORD in the land of the living! Wait for the LORD; be strong, and let your heart take courage; yea, wait for the LORD!

Psalm 29:3–4

The voice of the LORD is upon the waters; the God of glory thunders, the LORD, upon many waters. The voice of the LORD is powerful, the voice of the LORD is full of majesty.

Psalm 30:4–5

Sing praises to the LORD, O you his saints, and give thanks to his holy name. For his anger is but for a moment, and his favor is for a lifetime. Weeping may tarry for the night, but joy comes with the morning.

Psalm 31:3–5

Yea, thou art my rock and my fortress; for thy name's sake lead me and guide me, take me out of the net which is hidden for me, for thou art my refuge. Into thy hand I commit my spirit; thou hast redeemed me, O LORD, faithful God.

Psalm 32:5

I acknowledged my sin to thee, and I did not hide my iniquity; I said, "I will confess my transgressions to the LORD"; then thou didst forgive the guilt of my sin.

Psalm 33:6

By the word of the Lord the heavens were made, and all their host by the breath of his mouth.

Psalm 33:13–15

The LORD looks down from heaven, he sees all the sons of men; from where he sits enthroned he looks forth on all the inhabitants of the earth, he who fashions the hearts of them all, and observes all their deeds.

Psalm 34:18

The LORD is near to the brokenhearted, and saves the crushed in spirit.

Psalm 36:7–9

How precious is thy steadfast love, O God! The children of men take refuge in the shadow of thy wings. They feast on the abundance of thy house, and thou givest them drink from the river of thy delights. For with thee is the fountain of life; in thy light do we see light.

Psalm 37:3–5

Trust in the LORD, and do good; so you will dwell in the land, and enjoy security. Take delight in the LORD, and he will give you the desires of your heart. Commit your way to the LORD; trust in him, and he will act.

Psalm 37:23–24

The steps of a man are from the LORD, and he establishes him in whose way he delights; though he fall, he shall not be cast headlong, for the LORD is the stay of his hand.

Psalm 38:9–10

LORD, all my longing is known to thee, my sighing is not hidden from thee. My heart throbs, my strength fails me; and the light of my eyes—it also has gone from me.

Psalm 38:15

But for thee, O LORD, do I wait; it is thou, O LORD my God, who wilt answer.

Psalm 39:3–4

My heart became hot within me. As I mused, the fire burned; then I spoke with my tongue: "LORD, let me know my end, and what is the measure of my days; let me know how fleeting my life is!"

Psalm 40:5

Thou hast multiplied, O LORD my God, thy wondrous deeds and thy thoughts toward us; none can compare with thee! Were I to proclaim and tell of them, they would be more than can be numbered.

Psalm 43:3

Oh send out thy light and thy truth; let them lead me, let them bring me to thy holy hill and to thy dwelling!

Psalm 49:1–3

Hear this, all peoples! Give ear, all inhabitants of the world, both low and high, rich and poor together! My mouth shall speak wisdom; the meditation of my heart shall be understanding.

Psalm 50:10–11

For every beast of the forest is mine, the cattle on a thousand hills. I know all the birds of the air, and all that moves in the field is mine.

Psalm 51:6

Behold, thou desirest truth in the inward being; therefore teach me wisdom in my secret heart.

Psalm 51:12

Restore to me the joy of thy salvation, and uphold me with a willing spirit.

Psalm 51:15

O Lord, open thou my lips, and my mouth shall show forth thy praise.

Psalm 54:4

Behold, God is my helper; the Lord is the upholder of my life.

Psalm 56:3–4

When I am afraid, I put my trust in thee. In God, whose word I praise, in God I trust without a fear. What can flesh do to me?

Psalm 57:7–9

My heart is steadfast, O God, my heart is steadfast! I will sing and make melody! Awake, my soul! Awake, O harp and lyre! I will awake the dawn! I will give thanks to thee, O Lord, among the peoples; I will sing praises to thee among the nations.

Psalm 61:1–3

Hear my cry, O God, listen to my prayer; from the end of the earth I call to thee, when my heart is faint. Lead me to the rock that is higher than I; for thou art my refuge, a strong tower against the enemy.

Psalm 62:11–12

Once God has spoken; twice have I heard this: that power belongs to God; and that to thee, O Lord, belongs steadfast love. For thou dost requite a man according to his work.

Psalm 65:9

Thou visitest the earth and waterest it, thou greatly enrichest it; the river of God is full of water; thou providest their grain, for so thou hast prepared it.

Psalm 66:4–5

"All the earth worships thee; they sing praises to thee, sing praises to thy name." Come and see what God has done: he is terrible in his deeds among men.

Psalm 69:2–3

I sink in deep mire, where there is no foothold; I have come into deep waters, and the flood sweeps over me. I am weary with my crying; my throat is parched. My eyes grow dim with waiting for my God.

Psalm 69:5

O God, thou knowest my folly; the wrongs I have done are not hidden from thee.

Psalm 71:5–6

For thou, O Lord, art my hope, my trust, O LORD, from my youth. Upon thee I have leaned from my birth; thou art he who took me from my mother's womb. My praise is continually of thee.

Psalm 71:14–15

But I will hope continually, and will praise thee yet more and more. My mouth will tell of thy righteous acts, of thy deeds of salvation all the day, for their number is past my knowledge.

Psalm 72:5–7

May he live while the sun endures, and as long as the moon, throughout all generations! May he be like rain that falls on the mown grass, like showers that water the earth! In his days may righteousness flourish, and peace abound, till the moon be no more!

Psalm 73:25–26

Whom have I in heaven but thee? And there is nothing upon earth that I desire besides thee. My flesh and my heart may fail, but God is the strength of my heart and my portion for ever.

Psalm 75:6–7

For not from the east or from the west and not from the wilderness comes lifting up; but it is God who executes judgment, putting down one and lifting up another.

Psalm 77:11–13

I will call to mind the deeds of the LORD; yea, I will remember thy wonders of old. I will meditate on all thy work, and muse on thy mighty deeds. Thy way, O God, is holy. What god is great like our God?

Psalm 77:16–18

When the waters saw thee, O God, when the waters saw thee, they were afraid, yea, the deep trembled. The clouds poured out water; the skies gave forth thunder; thy arrows flashed on every side. The crash of thy thunder was in the whirlwind; thy lightnings lighted up the world; the earth trembled and shook.

Psalm 78:1–3

Give ear, O my people, to my teaching; incline your ears to the words of my mouth! I will open my mouth in a parable; I will utter dark sayings from of old, things that we have heard and known, that our fathers have told us.

Psalm 85:8

Let me hear what God the LORD will speak, for he will speak peace to his people, to his saints, to those who turn to him in their hearts.

Psalm 86:2–4

Preserve my life, for I am godly; save thy servant who trusts in thee. Thou art my God; be gracious to me, O Lord, for to thee do I cry all the day. Gladden the soul of thy servant, for to thee, O Lord, do I lift up my soul.

Psalm 86:6–7

Give ear, O LORD, to my prayer; hearken to my cry of supplication. In the day of my trouble I call on thee, for thou dost answer me.

Psalm 86:11–12

Teach me thy way, O LORD, that I may walk in thy truth; unite my heart to fear thy name. I give thanks to thee, O Lord my God, with my whole heart, and I will glorify thy name for ever.

Psalm 89:1–2

I will sing of thy steadfast love, O Lord, for ever; with my mouth I will proclaim thy faithfulness to all generations. For thy steadfast love was established for ever, thy faithfulness is firm as the heavens.

Psalm 89:14

Righteousness and justice are the foundation of thy throne; steadfast love and faithfulness go before thee.

Psalm 89:24

My faithfulness and my steadfast love shall be with him, and in my name shall his horn be exalted.

Psalm 90:14

Satisfy us in the morning with thy steadfast love, that we may rejoice and be glad all our days.

Psalm 95:4–5

In his hand are the depths of the earth; the heights of the mountains are his also. The sea is his, for he made it; for his hands formed the dry land.

Psalm 96:6

Honor and majesty are before him; strength and beauty are in his sanctuary.

Psalm 96:11–13

Let the heavens be glad, and let the earth rejoice; let the sea roar, and all that fills it; let the field exult, and everything in it! Then shall all the trees of the wood sing for joy before the

LORD, for he comes, for he comes to judge the earth. He will judge the world with righteousness, and the peoples with his truth.

Psalm 100:3

Know that the LORD is God! It is he that made us, and we are his; we are his people, and the sheep of his pasture.

Psalm 104:10–11

Thou makest springs gush forth in the valleys; they flow between the hills, they give drink to every beast of the field; the wild asses quench their thirst.

Psalm 104:24

O Lord, how manifold are thy works! In wisdom hast thou made them all; the earth is full of thy creatures.

Psalm 104:27–30

These all look to thee, to give them their food in due season. When thou givest to them, they gather it up; when thou openest thy hand, they are filled with good things. When thou hidest thy face, they are dismayed; when thou takest away their breath, they die and return to their dust. When thou sendest forth thy Spirit, they are created; and thou renewest the face of the ground.

Psalm 104:28

When thou givest to them, they gather it up; when thou openest thy hand, they are filled with good things.

Psalm 104:33–34

I will sing to the LORD as long as I live; I will sing praise to my God while I have being. May my meditation be pleasing to him, for I rejoice in the LORD.

Psalm 116:5–9

Gracious is the LORD, and righteous; our God is merciful. The LORD preserves the simple; when I was brought low, he saved me. Return, O my soul, to your rest; for the LORD has dealt bountifully with you. For thou hast delivered my soul from death, my eyes from tears, my feet from stumbling; I walk before the LORD in the land of the living.

Psalm 119:4–5

Thou hast commanded thy precepts to be kept diligently. O that my ways may be steadfast in keeping thy statutes!

Psalm 121:8

The LORD will keep your going out and your coming in from this time forth and for evermore.

Psalm 122:8

For my brethren and companions' sake I will say, "Peace be within you!"

Psalm 133:1

Behold, how good and pleasant it is when brothers dwell in unity!

Psalm 139:1–6

O LORD, thou hast searched me and known me! Thou knowest when I sit down and when I rise up; thou discernest my thoughts from afar. Thou searchest out my path and my lying down, and art acquainted with all my ways. Even before a word is on my tongue, lo, O LORD, thou knowest it altogether. Thou dost beset me behind and before, and layest thy hand upon me. Such knowledge is too wonderful for me; it is high, I cannot attain it.

Psalm 139:7–10

Whither shall I go from thy Spirit? Or whither shall I flee from thy presence? If I ascend to heaven, thou art there! If I make my bed in Sheol, thou art there! If I take the wings of the morning and dwell in the uttermost parts of the sea, even there thy hand shall lead me, and thy right hand shall hold me.

Psalm 139:16

Thy eyes beheld my unformed substance; in thy book were written, every one of them, the days that were formed for me, when as yet there was none of them.

Psalm 139:23–24

Search me, O God, and know my heart! Try me and know my thoughts! And see if there be any hurtful way in me, and lead me in the way everlasting!

Psalm 143:5–6

I remember the days of old, I meditate on all that thou hast done; I muse on what thy hands have wrought. I stretch out my hands to thee; my soul thirsts for thee like a parched land.

Psalm 143:8

Let me hear in the morning of thy steadfast love, for in thee I put my trust. Teach me the way I should go, for to thee I lift up my soul.

Psalm 145:5–7

On the glorious splendor of thy majesty, and on thy wondrous works, I will meditate. Men shall proclaim the might of thy terrible acts, and I will declare thy greatness. They shall pour forth the fame of thy abundant goodness, and shall sing aloud of thy righteousness.

Psalm 145:8

The Lord is gracious and merciful, slow to anger and abounding in steadfast love.

Psalm 145:9–10

The Lord is good to all, and his compassion is over all that he has made. All thy works shall give thanks to thee, O Lord, and all thy saints shall bless thee!

Psalm 145:14–16

The LORD upholds all who are falling, and raises up all who are bowed down. The eyes of all look to thee, and thou givest them their food in due season. Thou openest thy hand, thou satisfiest the desire of every living thing.

Psalm 147:5

Great is our Lord, and abundant in power; his understanding is beyond measure.

Psalm 147:7–8

Sing to the LORD with thanksgiving; make melody to our God upon the lyre! He covers the heavens with clouds, he prepares rain for the earth, he makes grass grow upon the hills.

Psalm 148:2–3

Praise him, all his angels, praise him, all his host! Praise him, sun and moon, praise him, all you shining stars!

Recommended Reading

Al-Halveti, S. (1985). *The Most Beautiful Names.* Putney, VT: Threshold Books.

Ali, A. Y. (2007). Holy Qur'an. Bensenville, IL: Lushena Books.

Ali, M. M. (1991). Holy Qur'an. Ahmadiyya Anjuman Ishaat.

Baker, R. (1999). *Merton & Sufism: The Untold Story: A Complete Compendium.* Louisville, KY: Fons Vitae.

Batchelor, S. (1998). *Buddhism Without Beliefs: A Contemporary Guide to Awakening.* New York, NY: Riverhead Books.

Chittick, W. C. (2000). *Sufism.* Oxford, UK: Oneworld.

Cutsinger, J. S. (2002). *Paths to the Heart: Sufism and the Christian East.* Bloomington, IN: World Wisdom.

De Caussade, J. (1981). *The Sacrament of the Present Moment.* New York, NY: HarperOne.

De Mello, A. (1985). *One Minute Wisdom.* New York, NY: DoubleDay.

Douglas-Klotz, N. (2003). *The Genesis Meditations: A Shared Practice of Peace for Christians, Jews, and Muslims.* Wheaton, IL: Quest Books, The Theosophical Publishing House.

Douglas-Klotz, N. (2005). *The Sufi Book of Life: 99 Pathways of the Heart for the Modern Dervish.* New York, NY: Penguin.

Epstein, M. (2004). *Thoughts Without A Thinker: Psychotherapy from a Buddhist Perspective.* New York, NY: MJF Books.

Glassman, B. (1996). *Instructions to the Cook: A Zen Master's Lessons in Living a Life that Matters.* New York, NY: Bell Tower.

Glassman, B. (1999). *Bearing Witness: A Zen Master's Lessons in Making Peace.* New York, NY: Bell Tower.

Gunn, R. J. (2000). *Journeys into Emptiness: Dogen, Merton, Jung and the Quest for Transformation.* New York, NY: Paulist Press.

Hafiz and D. Ladinsky (1999). *The Gift.* New York, NY: Penguin Compass.

Hafiz and D. Ladinsky (2006). *I Heard God Laughing: Poems of Hope and Joy.* New York, NY: Penguin.

HH The Dalai Lama. (2010). *Toward a True Kinship of Faiths: How the World's Religions Can Come Together.* New York, NY: Three Rivers Press.

Hliboki, J. (2011). *The Breath of God: Thirty-Three Invitations to Embody Holy Wisdom.* Atlanta, GA: Transilient Publishing.

Hughes, A. M. (2005). *Five Voices Five Faiths: An Interfaith Primer.* Lanham, MD: Cowley Publications.

Khan, H. I. (1989). *The Art of Being and Becoming.* New Lebanon, NY: Omega Press.

Khan, P.V. I. (1999). *Awakening.* New York, NY: Penguin.

Nasr, S. H. (2008). *The Garden of Truth: The Vision and Promise of Sufism, Islam's Mystical Tradition.* New York, NY: HarperOne.

Pearson, P. M. (2007). *Merton & Buddhism: Wisdom, Emptiness & Everyday Mind*. Louisville, KY: Fons Vitae.

Revised Standard Version Bible, Second Catholic Edition (2009). Ft. Collins, CO: Ignatius Press.

Salzberg, S. (2002). *Lovingkindness: The Revolutionary Art of Happiness*. Boston, MA: Shambhala Press.

Smith, H. (2009). *The World's Religions*. New York, NY: Harper-One.

Starr, M. (2012). *God of Love: A Guide to the Heart of Judaism, Christianity and Islam*. Rhinebeck, NY: Monkfish Book Publishing Company.

About the Author

Julie Hliboki, DMin, MA, is a certified professional coach, expressive arts educator, and interfaith spiritual director. Using creative arts, Julie works with individuals and groups to deepen into their own presence of compassion. This often leads to a greater acceptance of self and others, a more fully and effective engagement with the world, and an awareness of the Beloved in all.

Julie is the founder of the 99 Names Peace Project, the author of *The Breath of God: Thirty-Three Invitations to Embody Holy Wisdom,* and leads gatherings, workshops, and retreats that cultivate compassion. She lives in Atlanta with her beloved, David.

For more information, please visit:
www.JulieHliboki.com